Produced by
Mainstream Missouri Baptists

D1368015

FUNDAMENTALIST TAKEOVER IN THE SOUTHERN BAPTIST CONVENTION

A BRIEF HISTORY

by Rob James and Gary Leazer
with James Shoopman

1999 Edition

MEDIA

CIP
JAMES, ROB
   **The fundamentalist takeover in the southern baptist
convention: a brief history** / Rob James, Gary Leazer, James
Shoopman. Timisoara: Impact Media, 1999
       p. ; cm.
       ISBN 973 ~ 98677 ~ 1 ~ 5

I. Leazer, Gary
II. Shoopman, James
286

1999, **Impact Media**, Timisoara, Romania

http://www.impact-media.org; office@im.dnttm.ro

Printed in Romania.

EDITOR'S FOREWARD
by Dr. James G. Shoopman

At the 1999 winter meeting of the Cooperative Baptist Fellowship of Florida, I was asked to further refine and update *The Takeover of the Southern Baptist Convention*. In doing so I become the third editor, and this is the second major revision of this very useful work. The booklet was first produced in 1989. It had its beginnings in a report of the Denominational Relations Committee of River Road Baptist Church in Richmond, Virginia. Adding and reworking from that report, four authors worked together to produce the first edition of this work for a larger audience. They were Barbara Jackson, Robert E. Shepherd Jr., Cornelia Showalter and editor Robison B. (Rob) James. Dr. James did much of the final writing and re-writing, and so was listed on the front of the first editions as "editor."

A second updating of the book was produced under the auspices of *Baptists Today*, through the scholarship and editorial skills of Gary Leazer. Dr. Leazer had been an employee of the Home Mission Board, fired for explaining the Southern Baptist Convention's vote regarding Freemasonry to a masonic lodge meeting. Needless to say, Dr. Leazer was well acquainted with the events of the takeover and did a skillful job of updating the older work.

This latest presentation of the booklet is different in some small but significant ways. I was asked to make the work a little more lay person friendly, by eliminating some specialized language and explaining terms or ideas that might not be commonly known, except by Baptist historians. I provided some additional information for the sake of people who may not have followed the controversy while it was going on, and eliminated some portions of recent convention history that do not directly impinge upon the story of the fundamentalist takeover. I also occasionally rewrote sentences for greater clarity. Finally, I have taken the liberty of writing an introduction that clearly delineates the nature of the conflict and terms used to describe the conflict. I have also provided, in the introduction, a chronology of major incidents in the takeover history, so readers will have a brief overview of the tragic events described in this booklet, in the order of their occurrence. Section 25, "The Moderate Response to Fundamentalist Politics" is also new to this edition.

This work is an excellent tool for helping people understand what has happened to the Southern Baptist Convention over the last twenty years. If my small contribution has made it any clearer to the average reader, I am grateful for the opportunity to help fellow Christians toward a better understanding of the truth. The real credit for this work still belongs to the initial authors and the editors, Rob James and Gary Leazer, who did the original research and writing. I have made every effort to preserve the integrity and the spirit of their work. I pray the blessing of the Holy Spirit, who will guide us into all truth, for all who read this booklet.

INTRODUCTION
by Dr. James G. Shoopman, Editor

The purpose of this booklet is to inform readers about the history of important changes that have occurred in the Southern Baptist Convention over the last twenty years. The thesis of this work is that fundamentalist leaders in the Southern Baptist Convention organized and carried out a political campaign that has changed the character of the Southern Baptist Convention, and not for the better... It is our conviction that many good and well-intentioned conservatives were misled by this political activity. The goal of this misleading campaign was to place extreme fundamentalists in the seat of power and to drive out of the convention those who think differently from fundamentalists. The writers and editors of this volume believe:

1) that this campaign has changed the character of our convention, from one of openness to one of restricted thought, from one of spiritual liberty to one of fear to differ from the leadership.

2) that the political campaign has been carried out in a sinful and mean-spirited fashion, using innuendo, glittering generalities and exaggerations (all the usual tools of worldly politics) to achieve the ends of power.

3) that resulting changes have defied the perfect will of God, while hurting fellow Christians and defaming the noble tradition of what it means to be Baptist.

The reader should know that this work has been written and edited by traditional Baptists who accept Jesus Christ as personal Lord and Savior. We honor the Holy Bible as the sacred and divinely inspired word of God, and we believe in the Priesthood of all believers: meaning that all Christians are free under God to interpret the scripture according to their conscience and according to the best in Biblical scholarship.

The political campaign described in this book was launched by fundamentalists on the charge that the seminaries and denominational agencies were dominated by liberals. Using innuendo, exaggerations and glittering generalities, Fundamentalist leaders often implied a meaning for that word far from the truth about seminary professors and denominational executives. If you mean by a "liberal" someone who:

1) does not believe in the divine inspiration or spiritual truth value of the Bible,

2) does not believe in the divinity of Jesus,

3) does not believe in salvation by grace through faith in Christ,

if that is your image of a liberal, you may rest assured there were never many true liberals in the Southern Baptist Convention. To put it another way, if a lion that ate liberals was set loose in Southern Baptist institutions prior to the fundamentalist takeover, he would have soon starved to death.

This does not mean there were not serious disagreements between some seminary professors and some fundamentalist leaders, and the fundamentalists may have seen these as dangerous disagreements. It is, however, another thesis of this booklet that in the larger context of all Christian churches, the theological differences between Baptists were never so great that all Baptists could not have continued working together. Fundamentalist leaders in the Southern Baptist Convention forced the issue, demanding a fight, but not as a matter of theological debate. Rather, they turned their disagreements into a political conflict for power.

I have said there were few "real" liberals in the SBC prior to the takeover. This does not mean that there weren't some Baptists who were more "liberal" than others. Of course there were. Most of those who are more liberal than the fundamentalists would not call themselves "liberals," because in Baptist life the use of that word conjures up the unbelieving bogeyman described above. Rather, the persons responsible for this booklet prefer to refer to themselves as "moderates." It is impossible to tell the following story without using such terms, so it would be wise for the reader to know how we are using these words from the start.

First of all, its important to know what we are being conservative, moderate or liberal about. We are not talking about the politics of republicans and democrats. Perhaps the most useful way to define this would be to say that conservatives, moderates and liberals disagree on how much change there should be in traditional church teachings. The church teaches on a wide variety of subjects. Among them:

- The nature of God, the person of Christ and the work of the Holy Spirit,

- The nature of the Bible – its authorship, styles of study and interpretation,

- Marriage, divorce, sexuality, abortion, prayer in public schools, separation of church and state,

- The place of women in the workplace and the church.

Conservatives maintain that there should be little or no change in how the church teaches on these subjects, unless it is to make that teaching even more strict.

Liberals maintain there should be a great deal of change in how the church teaches on these subjects, usually in the direction of greater liberty, (thus connecting with the other definition of liberality – which is generosity.)

Moderates prefer a middle way, taking a more liberal approach to some things and a more conservative approach to others; that some teachings should change, and some teachings should stay the same. Moderates assume that newness or oldness does not make an idea good or bad. Instead, an idea is good or bad depending on whether it is consistent with the Bible, our conscience and sound study. If an idea is truthful and useful, it may lead to change, but not all "modern" ideas are good ideas, and not all "traditional" ideas are good either.

This, of course, still leaves us with the term, "fundamentalist." The most useful definition of a fundamentalist is a person who is angered by any liberal changes in the world or in church teaching. A fundamentalist is a person of very strict belief and behavior who requires absolute certainty about his/her beliefs, and is willing to fight for that certainty. A fundamentalist cannot abide any challenge to his beliefs either through the behavior or the beliefs of others. A fundamentalist is really a very specialized sort of conservative. Not all conservatives are fundamentalists, but all fundamentalists are extreme conservatives. They tend to regard any deviation from their norm as "dangerous." There are fundamentalists in all of the major world religions that have been affected by modernity, and each of them is characterized by anger at modernity, strict legalism and a desire to fight for more control of their environment.

This booklet tells the story of how fundamentalists in the Southern Baptist Convention carried out a fight for control of the denomination. Although they claimed this was a fight against dangerous "liberals" actually it was a fight to disenfranchise the moderates who later formed the Cooperative Baptist Fellowship, and the people who formed the Alliance of Baptists. The Alliance leaders are somewhat more liberal than their moderate counterparts in the CBF, but would not be considered genuinely liberal in any secular university religion department. There were no unbelieving bogeymen hidden in the closet of Southern Baptist leadership, but many good and effective Christian leaders have been driven from the institutions they loved and served with distinction because of the irrational and fanatical hatred set loose in the fundamentalist holy war. This booklet is the story of how that happened.

Events at the beginning and end of this conflict are described in chronological order, but most of the events in between are told in a slightly different fashion. The authors have chosen to tell much of the story in terms of how the changes in the convention affected each seminary and agency of the convention as the takeover progressed. So with the beginning of the conflict and the end described, you will then read of how the controversy in the convention affected first the Home Mission Board, then Southeastern Seminary and Southern Seminary, the Sunday School Board, the Foreign Mission Board and so on.

For that reason I have included in this introduction a chronology of some of the major events. To understand this chronology and the ensuing story, it is helpful to review a short glossary of names and abbreviations:

SBC: The Southern Baptist Convention. When referring to the annual meeting which determines denominational policy I will spell out the word, or refer to "the convention." When referring to it as a denominational entity I will usually use the abbreviation.

SBC Executive Board: In between annual meetings of the Southern Baptist Convention, necessary denominational business is carried on through occasional meetings of elected representatives to the Executive Board.

Alliance of Baptists: The first nationwide splinter group to organize moderates and more liberal Baptists outside the SBC., originally organized in 1986, as the "The Southern Baptist Alliance."

CBF: the **Cooperative Baptist Fellowship:** The second nationwide splinter group to organize moderate and conservative Baptists to do missions and ministry outside the SBC. They first met in 1990 and organized as the CBF in 1991.

HMB: the **Home Mission Board** of the Southern Baptist Convention, now called the North American Mission Board.

FMB: the **Foreign Mission Board** of the Southern Baptist Convention, now called the International Mission Board.

The six Southern Baptist Seminaries owned and operated by the Southern Baptist Convention in 1979 were:

> **Southern,** in Louisville, Kentucky.
>
> **Southeastern,** in Winston-Salem, North Carolina.
>
> **Southwestern:** in Forth Worth, Texas.
>
> **Midwestern:** in Kansas City, Missouri.
>
> **New Orleans:** in Louisiana.
>
> **Golden Gate:** in San Francisco, California.

Baptist Press: The original national/international Baptist news agency, serving the various state Baptist papers.

United Baptist Press: A new Baptist news agency to serve state and independent Baptist papers, formed after fundamentalists fired Baptist Press editors and began censoring Baptist Press.

CHRONOLOGY OF MAJOR EVENTS IN THE CONTROVERSY

1967: * Seminary Doctoral student Paige Patterson and Judge Paul Pressler meet at Café du Monde in New Orleans and discuss a long term strategy for fundamentalist domination of the Southern Baptist Convention.

1974 * The Baptist Faith and Message Fellowship identifies inerrancy of the Bible as the issue to be used in their struggle against moderates and liberals in the SBC.

1979 * Patterson, Pressler and others run a "get out the vote" campaign in 15 states prior to the Convention, urging a defeat of "liberalism" in the SBC.

* Voters are bussed to the convention in mass numbers but leave after the vote for president.

* Fundamentalist pastor Adrian Rogers is elected president.

1980 * Judge Pressler publicly announces the strategy of the fundamentalist takeover, which is to elect the SBC president a sufficient number of times to gain a fundamentalist majority on the boards and agencies of the Convention. This is to be accomplished through the president's power to make appointments. Pressler calls this, "Going for the jugular." [Trustee turnover is accomplished in 1989.]

1983 * SBC TODAY is launched as an independent Baptist paper with a moderate-friendly editorial approach.

1984 * A resolution against women pastors passes at the Kansas City Southern Baptist Convention.

* Paige Patterson announces that the Criswell institute is archiving recorded instances of liberalism. This is accomplished through students tape recording professors' lectures.

1985 * The Convention forms a " Peace Committee" to investigate the growing conflict and make recommendations for conflict resolution.

1986 * The Home Mission Board trustees become majority fundamentalist. The trustees bar women from receiving pastoral assistance in mission churches supported by HMB.

* The Southern Baptist Alliance is formed. (Becomes Alliance of Baptists in 1992.)

1987 * The Peace Committee report is adopted, recommending that hiring practices of boards and agencies reflect "the most commonly held beliefs" in the denomination. Moderates charge that Creedalism becomes official Convention policy through this action.

* The Southeastern Board of Trustees becomes majority fundamentalist. They take the Faculty out of the process for hiring new instructors, and place this power solely in hands of the president, who must use the Peace Committee document as a doctrinal guide for hiring.

* Randall Lolley, President of Southeastern Seminary, resigns in protest.

* HMB votes to forbid missionary appointment to persons who speak in tongues and divorced persons, unless the divorce falls within strict "Biblical guidelines."

1988 * HMB uses the Peace Committee report to enforce creedalism in hiring practices.

* The Southern Baptist Convention in San Antonio passes a resolution elevating strong pastoral authority. The resolution also denigrates the priesthood of all believers

* Richard Land, a fundamentalist leader, becomes President of the Christian Life Commission.

* The Foreign Mission Board fires moderate missionary Michael Willett after a fundamentalist missionary reports on Willett's opinions.

* Baptists Committed to the Southern Baptist Convention, a centrist group dedicated to convention loyalty, is formed in Texas.

1989 * Fundamentalist leaders give the Christian Life Commission greater responsibility for dealing with church/state issues, in order to circumvent working with the more moderate Baptist Joint Committee on Public Affairs.

1990 * Southern Seminary Board of Trustees becomes majority fundamentalist. Trustees give students permission to openly tape classes.

* Trustee Jerry Johnson of Colorado accuses Southern Seminary President Roy Honeycutt and many faculty of heresy.

* Baylor, Stetson Furman, and other Baptist colleges negotiate out of Baptist control.

* Baptist Press editors Al Shakleford and Dan Martin are fired by the SBC Executive Committee due to their reporting on the fundamentalist takeover effort and their refusal to cease writing such stories. Associated Baptist Press is formed in order to maintain a free press for Baptist news.

* Daniel Vestal calls a national level meeting of moderate Baptists in Atlanta. 3000 people show up and vow to meet again the next year. This will be the birth of the Cooperative Baptist Fellowship.

* Smyth & Helwys Publishing Company is founded for moderate Baptists of the south.

1991 * Southeastern Seminary publishes new statement of purpose and the doctrine of Biblical inerrancy becomes official policy.

* Moderate Sunday School Board President Lloyd Elder is forced to resign due to a hostile board of trustees. Fundamentalist leader Jimmy Draper becomes President of the Sunday School Board.

* The Foreign Mission Board votes to defund Rushlikon Seminary in Europe because of liberal professors.

* 6000 Baptists in Atlanta formally organize the Cooperative Baptist Fellowship.

* Moderates no longer offer an alternative candidate for President of the SBC.

1992 * Paige Patterson becomes President of Southeastern Seminary.

* Keith Parks, President of the Foreign Mission Board, resigns in protest against a hostile fundamentalist board of trustees. Parks becomes missions director for the Cooperative Baptist Fellowship.

1993 * Roy Honeycutt resigns as President of Southern Seminary due to a hostile fundamentalist board of trustees. Al Mohler, a leading fundamentalist, becomes President of Southern Seminary.

* The SBC votes to cease giving funds to the Baptist Joint Committee for Public Affairs, because it will not cooperate with the

fundamentalist agenda to restore publicly-led prayer in schools, government vouchers to attend religious schools and other right wing political/religious goals.

* Fundamentalists attempt to refuse seating for messengers from the church where President Clinton has his church membership.

* The Southern Baptist Convention affirms a report critical of membership in Freemasons.

* Gary Leazer is fired from the Home Mission Board for explaining the meaning of that vote to Masons at a Masonic meeting.

1994 * SBC Executive Committee leaders command SBC Seminaries to cease hosting booths at Cooperative Baptist Fellowship meetings.

* Moderate Professor Molly Marshall is forced to resign from Southern Seminary.

* A Hostile board of fundamentalist trustees at Southwestern Seminary fire President Russell Dilday and change the locks on his office.

* Ed Young, SBC President, calls for an end to "investigative reporting"

* Jim Henry is elected SBC President in Orlando at June Convention. He is the first president in several years elected who was not handpicked by the takeover faction. Although he pledged to support the inerrancy movement, his appointments were regarded by fundamentalists as "weak."

* Orlando convention votes to refuse CBF funds designated for Missionaries and other SBC agencies.

* In September the SBC executive Committee requests that State Conventions cut all ties to CBF. Not all state conventions have been compliant.

1995 * Diana Garland is fired as Dean of Carver School of Social work by Al Mohler.

* FMB President Jerry Rankin sends a letter to 40,000 pastors and Women's Missionary Union Directors, urging them to pray that the National WMU would cease cooperating with the CBF.

* John Jackson, then chair of the Board of Trustees for the FMB, compares the WMU's cooperation with the CBF with the acts of an adulterous woman.

1996 * The Florida Baptist Convention hires a legislative monitor.

* Southern Baptist Conservatives of Virginia form into rival state convention, in protest at the moderate nature of the existing state Association, which cooperates with the CBF and other moderate Baptists.

1997 * The Carver School of Social Work is cut from the curriculum at Southern Seminary and transferred to another college.

* Paul Debusman, librarian at Southern for 35 years, is fired over the content of a personal letter to Tom Eliff, then the SBC President.

* New Orleans seminary withdraws invitations to teach from two adjunct instructors due to their ties with the Cooperative Baptist Fellowship.

* The 1997 Southern Baptist Convention calls for a boycott of Disney Company and related companies, because of immorality in movies and business policies friendly to homosexuals.

1998 * There has been a 70% faculty turnover at Southern Seminary since 1991. Between 1992 and 1996, 42 employees had resigned, retired or were fired and three departments experienced complete turnover or loss of faculty.

* Jerry Falwell writes glowing endorsement of the fundamentalist takeover of the SBC.

* Fundamentalist Baptists in Texas formed Southern Baptists of Texas, to serve as a rival state convention in protest against the Baptist General Convention of Texas, which cooperates with various moderate Baptist organizations.

* The Southern Baptist Convention passes a new article on the family as an amendment to the Baptist Faith and Message statement of 1963. The amendment emphasizes female submission to the husband.

* Jerry Falwell attends a Southern Baptist Convention as a messenger for the first time.

* Paige Patterson, early leader of the fundamentalist takeover, is elected President of the Southern Baptist Convention.

1999 * SBC Messengers commission a panel to re-examine the Baptist Faith and Message Statement, with a view toward revising it to reflect "unambiguous" fundamentalist language.

* Paige Patterson elected to his second term as President of the SBC.

THE FUNDAMENTALIST TAKEOVER
IN THE SOUTHERN BAPTIST CONVENTION

Claiming sixteen million members in 41,000 churches, the Southern Baptist Convention (SBC) is the largest Protestant denomination in the United States. But as the media have made clear, the largest denomination is also the most troubled. For two decades, Southern Baptists have been caught up in one of the major denominational struggles of this century. Observers agree the struggle on the national level is over. Jack U. Harwell, editor (now retired) of SBC TODAY, wrote after the 1990 SBC in New Orleans:

> "The takeover is complete. Fundamentalists will control the SBC for the rest of this century, and beyond. The reality of finality was undeniable in the merciless juggernaut on the platform inside the Superdome."[1]

The question on the minds of thousands of Southern Baptists is: What happened?

At the heart of the struggle was a highly organized effort to take over the SBC and redirect it along lines that are "fundamentalist" in the classical sense of that term. The purpose of this brief history is to tell that story, and to tell it in such a way that it is clear, engaging, and easy to follow, whether the reader is familiar with the history of the Southern Baptist Convention and the recent controversy or knows next to nothing about it.

As will soon be apparent, however, important values are at stake in this story, values such as fair play, "soul freedom," church-state separation, "free cooperation rather than enforced conformity," and the full authority of the Bible, as distinct from the authority of someone's beliefs about the Bible.

The author of this book is not neutral about these values and the events of the past twenty years. He makes that fact clear at a number of points. If he had tried for strict, colorless neutrality, he would not only have stifled the significance of the facts; he would also have made a dramatic story dull and obscure. In an important sense, that would have been the ultimate injustice to the facts. For whatever else this story is, it certainly is not boring. None of this diminishes in any way his commitment to accuracy and fairness. He has gone out of his way to be fair and well-documented, and to avoid anything on the order of a personal attack.

1. Baptist Beginnings

While a few Southern Baptists attempt to trace Baptist beginnings back through J. M. Carroll's "Trail of Blood"[2], most historians agree that Baptist churches began as a protest during the reign of King James I of England (1566-1625). James I believed in the divine right of kings, the belief that kings received their authority to rule from God, rather than from the people. Those who protested or dissented from the king's claim were harassed, imprisoned, or forced to flee from England. Among those dissenters were John Smyth, Thomas Helwys,[3] and John Murton. These men called for separation from the Church of England, and thus earned the name "Separatists."

Smyth died in exile in Holland, while Helwys and Murton are credited with founding the first Baptist church on English soil in 1611 or 1612. Helwys would later die in prison for preaching that God alone, not the king, had authority over the souls of people.

Baptist John James was convicted of treason because he called Jesus Christ the King of England, Scotland, and Ireland. For his crime, James was hanged, drawn, and quartered in 1661.

Benjamin Keach, another Baptist pastor of the seventeenth century, was pilloried twice. Among his crimes was writing a book, *The Child's Instructor*, to teach children about the Christian faith. Keach was also criticized because he permitted women to sing in worship services when they were supposed to remain silent.

Religious liberty was the driving force behind the work of these early Baptists. Baptism of persons only after they have made a personal commitment to Jesus Christ as Lord and Savior has become one of the most basic Baptist beliefs. Even though these early Baptists rejected infant baptism, practiced in the Church of England, they generally tolerated those who held to a belief in that practice. In fact, persons holding both views could be found worshiping together in some Baptist churches.[4]

William Screven (1629-1713) of Kittery, Maine, is often credited as beginning the first Baptist church in the American South, although First Baptist Church, Charleston, South Carolina, had been organized fourteen years before Screven arrived in South Carolina. While in Maine, Screven was imprisoned for blasphemy, a charge arising from his teaching of believer's baptism.

The list of Baptists imprisoned in the American colonies for their beliefs seems endless. There was James Ireland, John Waller, Lewis Craig, James Reed, Allen Wyley, William Marsh, John Picket, Jeremiah Walker, and John Weatherford. Patrick Henry paid Weatherford's fine. Richard Furman was such a "notorious rebel" that a bounty of £1000 was placed on his head. Joseph Spencer's imprisonment on charges of "teaching and preaching the Gospel as a Baptist, not having license,"[5] led James Madison to urge a friend to "pray for liberty of conscience of all."[6] Madison would later be instrumental in the wording of A *Declaration of Rights*, adopted by the Virginia Convention in 1776.

That religion, or the duty which we owe to our Creator, and the manner of discharging it, can be directed only by reason and conviction, not by force or violence, and therefore all men are equally entitled to the free exercise of religion according to the dictates of conscience; and that it is the mutual duty of all to practice Christian forbearance, love and charity towards each other.[7]

John Leland wrote in *The Rights of Conscience*:

Every man must give an account of himself to God, and therefore every man ought to be at liberty to serve God in the way that he can best reconcile it to his conscience. If government can answer for individuals at the day of judgment, let men be controlled by it in religious matters, otherwise let me be free. It would be sinful for a man to surrender that to man, which is to be kept sacred for God.[8]

---

2. Two Visions In Conflict

The famed Southern Baptist unity in the past has been more functional than theological. Southern Baptists have banded together to minister in missions, evangelism, and Christian education. So long as they emphasize functional ministry, the "rope of sand," as one called it, holds; when they switch from function to doctrine, unity is threatened.
— Baptist historian H. Leon McBeth

The Southern Baptist Convention began by building on the foundation laid by earlier, freedom-loving Baptists. When the SBC was formed in 1845, the founders issued the following statement: "We have constructed for our basis no new creed; acting in this matter upon a Baptist aversion for all creeds but the Bible." A creed is an authoritative statement of doctrinal belief. Baptists have generally avoided creeds in the past because "authoritative" statements always invest "authority" in someone other than the believer–usually a denominational or governmental authority. The creed becomes a list of beliefs one must subscribe to in order to belong, and can be used against a believer who does not conform to the demands of the authorities. Instead of creeds,

Baptists have historically used "confessions of faith." Confessions are usually arrived at by group consensus, rather than handed down by higher authorities, and are not used to enforce conformity. They simply describe what the confessors already agree upon. Confessions of faith were preferred because "creeds" had been used against Baptists all too often in Europe and in the days of the colonies.

If not a creed, then what would be the basis for unity in the new denomination? In words that are still found in the preamble to the SBC constitution, the 1845 founders said the Convention they were creating was "a plan for eliciting, combining, and directing the energies of the denomination in one sacred effort, for the propagation of the Gospel."[9]

Those words identified the unifying principle of the SBC as a cooperative effort toward evangelism and missions. Sharing the gospel remained the unifying drive of the convention for the first 153 years of its life. It has hardly been better explained than in two lectures in 1980-81 delivered by the Baptist historian Walter B. Shurden, then dean and professor at Southern Baptist Theological Seminary in Louisville, Kentucky, and now Callaway Professor of Christianity and the chair of the Department of Christianity at Mercer University in Macon, Georgia.[10]

As Shurden put it, "...the new denomination was not to be united by theological uniformity." The unifying reality, he explained, "was missionary, not doctrinal, in nature."[11]

It was no small achievement to unify Baptists in the South. As Shurden points out, the SBC came together as a synthesis of four diverse traditions; the traditions of Charleston (South Carolina), Sandy Creek (North Carolina), Georgia, and Tennessee.

H. Leon McBeth, Distinguished Professor of Church History at Southwestern Baptist Theological Seminary in Fort Worth, Texas, emphatically agrees with Shurden's analysis.

The famed Southern Baptist unity in the past has been more functional than theological. Southern Baptists have banded together to minister in missions, evangelism, and Christian education. So long as they emphasize functional ministry, the "rope of sand," as one called it, holds; when they switch from function to doctrine, unity is threatened.[12]

In other words, the unity of the SBC is basically functional rather than doctrinal.

Almost the opposite view was asserted in February 1988 by four SBC presidents who had been elected by the takeover movement from 1979 to 1987. In a formal statement, they declared their commitment to "doctrinal unity in functional diversity."[13] In a strong break from the past, they placed strict doctrinal uniformity ahead of cooperation in the mission.

These are the two conflicting visions about what unifies Southern Baptists. The collision between these two visions has been the essence of the struggle among Southern Baptists since 1979.

3. The Roots of Fundamentalism

"I feel if J. Frank Norris were here today and saw the direction the SBC was moving, he would vote with us to reunite with Southern Baptists. This is an effort to complete the fight for the Bible started under Norris."
— Billy Ramsey, pastor, First Baptist Church, Ft. Worth, Texas.

The roots of the historic Southern Baptist vision are clear. What are the roots of the contrasting vision expressed by the four recent SBC presidents? What was the vision that drove the takeover effort? More importantly we ask: To what extent is the takeover vision of the SBC a fundamentalist vision?

Leon McBeth, whom we have already quoted, is one of the most distinguished Baptist historians in the world. His 850-page *Baptist Heritage* of 1987 is a standard textbook. He frankly characterizes the takeover faction in the SBC as "fundamentalist."

"I intend nothing pejorative in applying the term to contemporary Southern Baptists who espouse ultraconservative theological and social views," McBeth says. But he continues, "Fundamentalism, in whatever religious group, tends to be unable to tolerate diversity and often seems determined to 'rule or ruin' its group."[14]

Duke University church history professor George W. Marsden, author of two books on American fundamentalism, defines a Christian fundamentalist as "an evangelical Protestant who is militantly opposed to modern liberal theologies and to some aspects of secularism in modern culture."[15] Baptist sociologist Nancy Ammerman contends that fundamentalism is a mindset or "a way of life that transcends any other institution that might make claims on an individual."[16]

Contrary to claims made that fundamentalism represents historic biblical faith, fundamentalism is a recent phenomenon. The fundamentalist mindset can be traced back only to the late nineteenth century when certain Christians began to be concerned about trends in religious belief. It achieved its militant, ultra-conservative character and identity in reaction against evolutionary ideas, the historical-critical study of the Bible, and liberal or "modernist" theology. At the Niagara Bible Conference in 1895, these Christians defined their position with a specific set of doctrinal affirmations: (1) the authority and inerrancy of Scripture; (2) the Virgin Birth and deity of Christ; (3) Christ's substitutionary atonement; (4) Christ's physical resurrection; and (5) the Second Coming and his earthly, millennial reign.

While these beliefs were shared by many Christians, fundamentalists turned these affirmations into a kind of creed, and sought to discredit any Christian leader who disagreed with their interpretation of these doctrines, in even the smallest point.

Between 1910 and 1915, a series of twelve small volumes, *The Fundamentals: A Testimony to the Truth*, was published. Three million copies of the booklets were mailed to every Christian minister and theology student whose address could be obtained. Due to the impact of this series, the term "fundamentalist" was coined in 1920.[17]

In the 1920s, fundamentalists fought a war on primarily two fronts, a war that in essential respects was reopened in the 1970s and 1980s.[18] On one front of their war in the 1920s, fundamentalists entered the political arena in an effort to outlaw the teaching of evolution in public schools. The campaign fell apart after the famous Scopes "monkey trial" of 1925 in Dayton, Tennessee.

On the other front of their war, fundamentalists attempted to purge or take over several Protestant denominations, especially the Northern Baptist and Northern Presbyterian denominations. (There were virtually no liberals in the SBC, and probably not many moderates, so it was not extensively affected by the classic conflict of the 1920s.)

On the denominational front of their war, fundamentalists used lists of "fundamental" doctrines as tests of orthodoxy. The lists were not always identical, but usually included the affirmations of the 1895 Niagara Bible Conference. All lists included substantially the following statement: The Bible, at least in its original manuscripts, is both infallible (incapable of error) or inerrant (generally said to mean error-free in areas of faith, history, and geography), and inspired by God, word for word.

By the 1930s, the fundamentalists had also lost in their struggle to take over various denominations. A middle or centrist group was in charge of the Northern denominations, a group that was neither modernist (liberal) nor fundamentalist. The liberals had not been expelled, however, and the centrist group was far too broad to suit the fundamentalists. Not willing to be "yoked together" with that kind of diversity, they began splitting off and forming their own independent groups.[19]

This sustained experience of militant struggle has bred into the sprawling fundamentalist movement a powerful tendency (a "fundamentalist gene," so to speak) to be narrowly creedal and separatist. Fundamentalist churches tend strongly toward independence. That is, they do not line up easily with a denomination. It is true that a large number of moderately fundamentalist churches have cooperated to various degrees with the SBC. But other fundamentalists have carried on open warfare.

The most colorful and spectacular example was J. Frank Norris, pastor of the First Baptist Church of Fort Worth, Texas. He was known for his sensationalist sermon topics, including "The Ten Biggest Devils in Fort Worth, Names Given." Norris shot a friend of the mayor of Fort Worth who came to his church office. Indicted for murder, Norris pleaded self-defense and was acquitted. When church trustees attempted to fire him, he fired all of the trustees and deacons. Six hundred members left the church, a move Norris viewed as a "purification process."[20]

From 1921 until his death in 1952, Norris, known as the "Texas tornado," engaged in vitriolic attacks on Southern Baptists, Baylor University, Texas Baptists, and the SBC.[21] He accused George W. Truett, pastor of the First Baptist Church of Dallas, of being under the control of modernists. Southwestern Seminary president L. R. Scarborough referred to "Norrisism" as a "cult."[22] Norris' church was expelled by Tarrant County Baptist Association, in which Fort Worth is located, in 1920 and by the Baptist General Convention of Texas in 1924. Norris' church remained within the SBC until 1948 when the Convention refused to seat him.

He formed the World Fundamental Baptist Mission Fellowship in 1938. The Fellowship's seminary, the Baptist Bible Institute in Fort Worth, opened the following year. John R. Rice, fundamentalist editor of the *Sword of the Lord* newsletter, and John Birch, after whom the John Birch Society is named, attended the seminary.

Mark Toulouse says of Norris, "Anyone who differed in any way with Norris immediately became a likely candidate for a tongue-lashing, if not something worse."[23] Also,

The only thing to which he was subject was his own undying passion to dominate. Few among his contemporaries could hold their own against his verbal attacks, for his conscience seemingly never interfered with his method. Any tactic was acceptable to him so long as it helped him to achieve his purposes, purposes that, to the consternation of his opponents, he sincerely viewed as synonymous with the purposes of God.[24]

First Baptist Church of Fort Worth voted in 1990 to rejoin the Southern Baptist Convention, in light of the denomination's move toward fundamentalism. Pastor Billy Ramsey explained the decision. "I feel if J. Frank Norris were here today and saw the direction the SBC was moving, he would vote with us to reunite with Southern Baptists. This is an effort to complete the fight for the Bible started under Norris."[25]

To understand this mindset, it is important to realize that fundamentalism is more than certain beliefs. Most Southern Baptists hold many and some hold all of the beliefs that are characteristic of fundamentalism. But that does not mean they are fundamentalists.

The key question is how militant and exclusive they are in insisting that others agree with them before they are willing to "do church" with them. As McBeth explains, fundamentalism is "at least as much a spirit and attitude as a set of theological beliefs."

4. What The Controversy Is About

We will now turn our attention to the recent Southern Baptist controversy.

On one side of the conflict, Southern Baptist traditionalists are struggling to ensure that those within the SBC can continue to work together to carry the saving gospel to the homeland and to the world, to educate, and to do benevolent work — and to do all this in a way that respects the freedom of their brothers and sisters in Christ, cherishes considerable diversity, and refrains from imposing narrow doctrinal tests.

On the other side of the struggle, the "fundamentalist gene" is present, the inbred tendency to be exclusive and to use narrow tests of orthodoxy in militant fashion. The takeover leadership are determined to make one human view of the Bible a prerequisite for anyone who would assume a leadership role within the SBC.

This contrast does not mean that mainstream Southern Baptist traditionalists have few convictions. Far from it. It means that Baptists have most often been united around Jesus Christ, rather than around this or that doctrine *about* Jesus Christ.

Likewise, with respect to the Bible, Baptists have most often been united around the Scriptures, rather than around this or that doctrine or theory *about* the Scriptures.

In 1987, James H. Slatton, pastor of the River Road Baptist Church in Richmond, Virginia, wrote, "Southern Baptists always have gathered around the Bible itself and not around theories about the Bible." Continuing in his one-page statement, Slatton said, "Our loyalty must be to the Scriptures, and not to human notions about the Scriptures."

The takeover leadership speaks regularly about taking the denomination back to its roots.[26] But as we have seen, they are trying to graft the denomination onto fundamentalist roots that are different from the roots from which the SBC actually grew.

5. The Campaign Begins: Houston, 1979

In June 1979, the annual meeting of the SBC was held in Houston, Texas. A few months earlier, Paul Pressler and Paige Patterson had announced that they and their colleagues were going to elect a "conservative" SBC president and restore the SBC to its "historical roots," as they put it.

Pressler, a state appeals court judge in Houston (now retired), and Patterson, then president of Criswell College in Dallas, had adopted an overall strategy for controlling the Convention. These two men had met years earlier while Patterson was a student at New Orleans Baptist Theological Seminary. In a late night meeting at the Café du Monde, a popular eatery in the French Quarter of New Orleans, the two men discussed what they believed was a liberal drift in the Convention. That 1967 meeting would forever change the history of the SBC and launch what would become known as the Pressler-Patterson coalition.[27]

Another late night meeting at the Café du Monde illustrated how successful was the campaign begun in 1979. In June 1990, again late at night, a group of about two dozen men sat eating beignets and drinking café au lait. One of the men climbed upon a table and announced to the customers that the group would sing "Victory in Jesus" to celebrate twelve years of victory over the moderates in the Southern Baptist Convention.

Pressler had proposed a political strategy to Patterson to elect a president in sympathy with their objectives. The president would, in turn, nominate like-minded people to the Convention's committee on committees. This committee would nominate like-minded people to the committee on nominations. This second committee would nominate like-minded trustees and directors to Southern Baptist agencies and institutions who would hire only like-minded staff. Pressler called this strategy, "going for the jugular."

We are going for the jugular. We are going for ...trustees of all our institutions, who are not going to sit there like a bunch of dummies and rubber stamp everything that's presented to them.[28]

Adrian Rogers, pastor of the Bellevue Baptist Church in Memphis, was selected by the Pressler-Patterson coalition as their candidate for President of the SBC in 1979. Pressler, Patterson, and others occupied a command post in "sky-boxes" above the convention floor and maintained contact with the floor beneath through an elaborate communications network.[29]

In a stunning development, Rogers was elected on the first ballot, even though there were six candidates, several of them very conservative. The victory was largely due to a large get-out-the-vote campaign Pressler and Patterson conducted in 15 states prior to the Convention.[30]

Fundamentalist candidates have won the Convention presidency every year since 1979, although Jim Henry was not the hand-picked candidate in 1994-1995. These presidents and the dates of their elections are:

Adrian Rogers	1979
Bailey Smith	1980, 1981
James Draper	1982, 1983
Charles Stanley	1984, 1985
Adrian Rogers	1986, 1987
Jerry Vines	1988, 1989
Morris Chapman	1990, 1991
Edwin Young	1992, 1993
Jim Henry	1994, 1995
Tom Eliff	1996, 1997
Paige Patterson	1998

6. Going For The Jugular

We are going for the jugular. We are going for ...trustees of all our institutions, who are not going to sit there like a bunch of dummies and rubber stamp everything that's presented to them. — Judge Paul Pressler

In the strictest sense, the Southern Baptist Convention exists for only a few days each year while the annual meeting is in session. The work of the Convention is done by staff who are employed by the approximately twenty agencies of the Convention.

The best known of these SBC agencies are the Foreign Mission Board (renamed the International Mission Board in 1997), the Home Mission Board (renamed the North American Mission Board in 1997), the six seminaries, and the Sunday School Board (renamed LifeWay Christian Resources in 1998), a huge self-supporting enterprise that publishes and markets literature mainly for Southern Baptists. More powerful, but probably less well known, is the SBC Executive Committee.

Each of these agencies and institutions are governed by trustees or directors nominated and elected by messengers to the annual meeting of SBC. These trustees set policy, adopt budgets, and employ or fire at least the top level of staff in their respective agencies or institutions. These individuals are the "jugular" to which Pressler referred in his often-quoted statement in 1980, "We are going for the jugular."

By early 1989, nearly every one of the SBC boards had a majority of takeover people on it. The Southern Baptist Theological Seminary in Louisville, Kentucky would not "tip over" until 1990. The Home Mission Board, the first agency to be taken over, had a majority of takeover directors by 1984.

How tightly committed to the Pressler-Patterson agenda were the people who made up these new majorities? Not all of them were in lock-step agreement, but it would appear that they were expected to vote in conformity with fundamentalist views only. An early 1989 editorial in the *Southern Baptist Advocate*, the voice of the Pressler-Patterson coalition, complained that some of those who "have been put on Boards and commissions ...are not voting with conservatives," that is, with the takeover faction.

The editorial continued, "if we fill vacancies with people who feel they have to be conciliatory to the liberals [that is, to moderate-conservatives], ...all our effort has been in vain." Set off in bold print in the editorial is the statement, "They don't seem to have any use for a Jesus who plaited a whip and drove a bunch of phonies out of the temple."[31]

7. The Anatomy Of A Takeover

How was it possible for the Pressler-Patterson group to accomplish their goal? As Pressler explained to Patterson over beignets at the Café du Monde, the key was the immense appointive powers concentrated in the office of the SBC president.

The SBC president is elected in June for a one-year term. He can be re-elected for one consecutive term. In the spring of the each year, about nine months after he is elected, the president appoints a committee on committees.

This 70-member committee on committees fulfills its responsibility several weeks later at the annual SBC meeting in June. At that time, it nominates (and the messengers elect) a second large committee, the all-important committee on nominations. (Until 1987, this committee was named "the committee on boards.")

This powerful committee shows its importance a year later at the next annual meeting of the SBC. At that time (two years after the election of the president who "stands behind it"), this committee nominates a person for every vacancy on every one of the twenty boards of trustees/directors that govern the Convention's agencies and institutions. (See diagram below.)

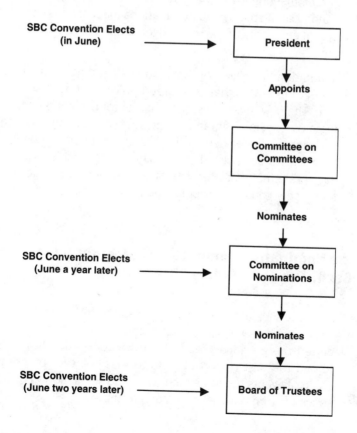

Not all trustees/directors are replaced in a single year. They serve staggered terms. Some terms are four years, while some are five years, depending upon the agency or institution. Trustees/directors may succeed themselves for a second term at the will of the committee on nominations. Normally they do. It could take ten years to completely recycle a board of trustees/directors. It requires several years to shift the majority on any given board, but a series of presidents can bring that change about if they each follow a single plan. That is precisely what happened.

While messengers at the annual meeting of the SBC elect the trustees/directors, the committee on nominations, almost without exception, dictates who will be elected. It's easy to understand why this would be so. The thousands of messengers at an annual meeting would be hard pressed to change more than a handful of the nearly 250 nominations made by this committee, even if a majority of the messengers wanted to do so. Sufficient time is not allowed.

In addition, a revision of Bylaw 16 pushed through by the takeover group in 1986 has centralized power even further than before. The new rule makes it still harder for a majority of the voting messengers at an annual meeting to make any changes in what has been decided by the committee prior to the Convention. The revised Bylaw 16 prohibits a messenger from nominating an alternative slate of trustees/directors from the floor. A messenger can only propose changes *one name at a time*.[32]

8. The Nominating Committee That Might Have Been: The 1985 Dallas SBC

Why was such a constrictive bylaw adopted in 1986? To answer that question, we will look at some dramatic events that occurred the previous year.[33] The 1985 Convention in Dallas afforded the best opportunity up to that point for breaking the chain of events the fundamentalists had set in motion with their series of "turn out the vote" campaigns.

When the committee on committees presented its report in Dallas, James Slatton of Richmond, Virginia, made an electrifying proposal. He moved that the messengers elect an alternate committee on nominations (then called the committee on boards). Slatton's alternate slate consisted of the various state convention presidents, plus the presidents of the state Woman's Missionary Unions. These people had been elected in their home states. Few of them would be sympathetic toward the takeover agenda. If the messengers had elected the alternate slate as the committee on nominations, these individuals would have nominated trustees/directors, generally of a "pre-1979 type," at the 1988 Convention.

Slatton said his motion was a way to peace. He was right. For at least one year — and the precedent might have been followed in subsequent years — his proposal would have removed the main reason for the annual pitched battle over electing a president. It would have gone far to "de-politicize" the presidency: moving to a state-selected committee on nominations would have taken much of the power concentrated in the SBC president and distributed it back to the grassroots.

Hindsight reveals an irony here. A peace committee was created in Dallas in 1985. It was supposed to determine the sources of the controversy and bring Southern Baptists together, but it did not. In the three years of its existence, the peace committee failed to bring peace to the Convention. By contrast, a Slatton-type committee on nominations would have been a real "peace committee," at least for a year, and quite possibly for much longer, as we have noted. But that step toward peace was destined to become one of history's "might have beens." How many times have Southern Baptists had the opportunity to bring peace to their denomination, but missed the opportunity?

When Slatton made his motion, Convention president Charles Stanley ruled, with the advice and assistance of parliamentarian Wayne Allen of Tennessee, that the substitute was out of order. Slatton's proposed nominees would have to be voted on one by one, he said. Slatton appealed Stanley's ruling. The messengers overruled Stanley by a vote of 12,576 to 11,801, affirming Slatton's position.

When the Convention reconvened that evening, however, Stanley had found a new basis for ruling against Slatton, not-withstanding the vote of the full convention to proceed with a vote on Slatton's motion. Stanley ruled that SBC Bylaw 16 prevented the messengers from amending the committee's slate of nominees. The slate, he ruled, must either be accepted or rejected as a whole.

At this point, multiple cries of "point of order" broke out at microphones all over the hall. Some, if not all, of those seeking to be recognized wanted to appeal Stanley's ruling once again. But, as the video record makes clear, Stanley moved quickly to force a vote, refusing to recognize anyone with contrary views. The committee's slate was accepted by a vote of 13,123 to 9,851. The Convention secretary, Lee Porter, observed that about 4,000 more ballots were cast than there appeared to be people in the hall. Porter still stands by that observation. Later on, a messenger from Alabama initiated a lawsuit so the validity of the vote could be investigated, but the courts refused to hear the case, citing the separation of church and state.

William J. Cumbie of Virginia, convention parliamentarian for three previous annual meetings, termed the rulings on this issue "bizarre." Although Bylaw 16 says the committee on committees "shall" nominate the committee on nominations, Bylaw 16 allows the messengers to amend all committee reports, Cumbie observed. This latter provision, he concluded, vested ultimate power in the messengers over all committee recommendations.

The revisions to Bylaw 16 were made a year after the Dallas SBC to ensure that no moderate majority could derail the takeover in the future. No repeats of the 1985 experience were wanted. It seemed clear to the moderates that the takeover faction wanted the reins of power to be held in very few hands. To insure that, the grassroots were not allowed to have input — or at least not the kind of input Slatton's "peace committee" would have given them.[34]

9. Stepping Stones To The "Inerrancy Controversy"

The takeover movement, as is well known, has gained most of its credibility by marching under the banner of "biblical inerrancy." Inerrancy is the affirmation that the Bible, in each and every part, is free of any error of any kind on any subject, geography, science, and history, as well as in its message of salvation and instruction for life. The fundamentalist community conceives of the Bible as dictated word for word by God. Since God cannot make mistakes, the Bible must therefore be inerrant.

The moderate faction conceives the Bible as being composed under the inspiration of the Holy Spirit, with the human writers as active participants with God in the work. Thus the Bible has a human face, but a divinely given heart. With that view in mind, most moderates prefer the ancient affirmation that the Bible is "the infallible rule of faith and practice." Moderates prefer not to use the term "inerrant" because serious Biblical scholarship clearly proves that the "human face" of scripture contains many a human flaw. Most moderates would agree that none of these flaws affect any Christian doctrine or historical affirmation. Nevertheless, moderates do not consider it wise to claim things for scripture that scripture does not claim for itself, and the Bible does not claim to be humanly inerrant. Moreover, moderates do not consider it honest to claim things for scripture that are simply not true. Moderates believe that the "divine heart" of scripture has ample power to demonstrate the Bible's inspiration and authority.

Fundamentalist scholars confess the existence of human flaws in scripture, but prefer to refer to these as "unresolved difficulties." They insist that the scholar's approach to scripture weakens the Bible's authority and thus weakens the power of Christian preaching. Therefore they have been quick to declare that anyone who will not describe the Bible as "inerrant" is a dangerous liberal who "does not believe the Bible." Using this rhetoric, fundamentalist leaders convinced the rank and file Baptists that the seminaries were filled with dangerous liberals who would corrupt the believing heart of the SBC from within. Thousands of frightened believers came to the conventions from 1979 to 1990 to save the convention from these evil scholars, when in fact our seminaries were filled with decent, believing professors who refused to lie about the Bible, even when their jobs were threatened by the fundamentalist movement.

To better understand the power that is packed into this "inerrancy issue," we will step back in time and see how inerrancy became a rallying point.[35] ..

In 1961, the Sunday School Board's book publishing house, Broadman Press (now called Broadman and Holman Publishers), published *The Message of Genesis*, by Midwestern Baptist Seminary professor Ralph Elliott. Not a radical work, nor intended to be, Elliott's work was a simple, straightforward survey and theological interpretation of Genesis. Elliot did, however, depart from the traditional teachings about Genesis common in many Baptist churches in at least two areas. Elliot believed Genesis was written by a number of different inspired writers, rather than following the traditional view that Moses wrote it. This has been the prevailing view in most academic study of Genesis for many years. Elliott also wrote that the first eleven chapters of Genesis were divinely intended as a symbolic account rather than as literal history.

The book created an unexpected furor. There were demands for its withdrawal and for the firing of the author. An SBC committee was appointed to write a new confession of faith for the SBC. The result was the current "Baptist Faith and Message" of 1963. No official action was taken against Elliott or the book, but Broadman Press decided against a second edition.

A special committee of Midwestern Seminary's trustees, with the seminary president, requested that Elliott not seek another publisher. Repeatedly, Elliott said he would not if so requested by the full board of trustees. The board made no such request. When the committee reported to the board that it was "impossible to come to a mutual working relationship" with Elliott, he was fired — not for heresy, but for insubordination![36]

The smoldering fires broke out again in 1969 over the publication of the first volume of *The Broadman Commentary*. The Genesis section was written by an English Baptist, G. Henton Davies, while the Exodus section was written by Roy L. Honeycutt, Jr., then at Midwestern Seminary and later president of Southern Seminary. The attack centered on the treatment of the Genesis story in which Abraham is told to sacrifice his son Isaac. The commentary suggested that this was Abraham's understanding of God's will, but may not have been God's instructions.[37]

When the Convention met in Denver in 1970, the sessions were stormy. After an acrimonious debate, a motion was passed, 5,394 to 2,170, to rewrite the volume with "due respect to the conservative point of view." The Sunday School Board planned to ask Davies to rewrite the commentary on Genesis. However, when the Convention met in 1971, a resolution demanding a new author write the Genesis commentary passed by a vote of 2,672 to 2,290. The Sunday School Board complied.[38] Southern Baptist Seminary professor Clyde T. Francisco was enlisted to write a new commentary on Genesis for *The Broadman Commentary*.[39]

Spurred on by these events, a group met at First Baptist Church, Atlanta, Georgia, in 1973 and formed the Baptist Faith and Message Fellowship to fight what they called "liberalism." The group launched *The Southern Baptist Journal*, and named William A. Powell, a Home Mission Board staff member, editor. Powell claimed that the paper slashed like a broad-axe in all directions against the "cancer of liberalism." Powell's personal attacks on denominational leaders led most of the *Journal's* board to resign, but he would not be dissuaded. By 1975, the *Journal*, published only as funds became available, began to lose some of its influence and support.

In 1976, Harold Lindsell's *The Battle for the Bible* was published. An immensely popular book, it reached its sixth printing early the next year. Lindsell, editor of the evangelical biweekly, *Christianity Today*, had spent most of his professional life in nondenominational circles.[40] Lindsell followed up with a rambling sequel, *The Bible in the Balance*, in 1979. The book was timed for release at the Houston SBC that year.

In these books, Lindsell, who had become president of the Baptist Faith and Message Fellowship, argued for a rigid form of belief in biblical inerrancy. He insisted that without strict inerrancy, Christian denominations decay. He neglected to rule out other possible causes of decline, and also neglected to mention Christian groups that had declined while they held to inerrancy. This line of thinking, with its dubious interpretation of history,[41] soon became one of the battle cries of the SBC takeover effort.

While Lindsell wrote mostly about other denominations, he gave considerable unfriendly attention to Southern Baptists. His books demonstrated how effective it can be to quote passages from a person's writings out of context, without regard to whether they were meant for a scholarly audience or for the laity. Lindsell's habit of misquoting writers led to more dangerous consequences when Pressler, Patterson, and others began to travel the country in the takeover effort. A number of the specific criticisms and quotations they hurled like hand grenades into the SBC controversy appear to have been lifted directly from Lindsell's books.[42]

Leon McBeth shows that, in the earlier Elliott and Broadman controversies, the term "inerrancy" was rarely used, even by ultraconservatives. He believes Lindsell's immensely popular *Battle for the Bible* catapulted "inerrancy" into common use among Southern Baptists. "One might even say," McBeth concludes, "that Lindsell moved the Southern Baptist controversy into this new stage of biblical inerrancy."[43]

McBeth appears to be correct. However, the term was deliberately introduced as a weapon in the fight two years earlier, as we shall see.

10. Is Inerrancy The Real Issue?

"We're going to do whatever it takes to take over the state convention and the SBC," explained M. O. Owens of North Carolina in 1970.[44] Owens, a founder of the Baptist Faith and Message Fellowship mentioned earlier in this book, continued, "We're going to organize the losers of every election and cause of Southern Baptist history we can identify."

"Under what special issue are you going to fly a flag?" James L. Sullivan, president of the Sunday School Board, asked Owens. "We haven't picked it yet," Owens answered, "but when we pick it, it will be one that no one can give rebuttal to without hopelessly getting himself into controversy." In 1974, as Sullivan narrated the events, *The Southern Baptist Journal* announced the issue would be inerrancy.

Sullivan's anecdote implies a larger role for the Owens group than they actually played in the takeover; but his account is highly suggestive of how the inerrancy issue *worked* in the controversy. The inerrancy issue has worked as a yes/no question like "Have you stopped beating your wife?" A moderate with any honesty cannot answer that question without *appearing* to lack faith in scripture's spiritual perfection, even though he or she believes in the Bible just as much as the fundamentalist questioner. The battle over inerrancy has also worked to distract people from hidden agendas, perhaps unconsciously, as people have used the emotional power of the issue to settle old feuds, to gain positions of power in the SBC, or — as a later section of this book will give reason to suspect — to achieve certain goals in national politics.

What about the inerrancy issue itself? Is it really the core issue that divides the people of the Southern Baptist Convention? Three reasons can be cited to demonstrate that beliefs about "inerrancy" did not divide Southern Baptists until the fundamentalist movement exaggerated the importance of the issue.. These reasons are spelled out by a team of scholars in *The Unfettered Word*, which was first published in 1987.[45] These three reasons were also set forward during a "Conference on Biblical Inerrancy" sponsored by the six SBC seminary presidents in 1987.[46] These three reasons have been set forth with the following arguments:

(1) Since the time of Lindsell's 1976 book (see above), fundamentalists have wrongly insisted that inerrancy is the definitive view of Southern Baptists.[47] The sources upon which takeover

people have based this unsound view of "our historic tradition" cannot be trusted at several key points.[48]

Three respected shapers of Southern Baptist theology, E. Y. Mullins, A. T. Robertson, and W. T. Conner, have been misinterpreted by takeover leaders. These three theologians rejected the kind of inerrancy position advocated by the leaders of the takeover movement,[49] and Mullins and Conner actively sought to counter such arguments. The takeover movement has treated these theologians with a mixture of ignorance and distortion that could be called a crime against historical knowledge.[50]

Many Southern Baptists have described themselves as inerrantists. Many Southern Baptists always will. But Southern Baptists have not "creedalized" that one human view of Scripture. They have insisted that the Bible itself is the final court of appeal, not someone's dogma about the Bible.[51]

The very cautious James Leo Garrett, Jr., professor of theology at Southwestern Seminary (now retired), states:

One must come to the twentieth century before one finds in Baptist confessions of faith an application of the term "infallible" to the inspiration of the Bible. Such an application is found exclusively in Landmark and Fundamentalist [not in Southern Baptist] confessions.[52]

Leon McBeth's comment about Southern Baptists is apt:

Their own theologians are almost unknown among them; their earlier confessions unfamiliar. This allows some Southern Baptists to claim recent innovations as "the historic Baptist position" on certain issues.[53]

---

(2) When fundamentalist leaders have attacked Southern Baptist scholars for not being inerrantists, they have ignored an important fact. They fail to mention that non-Southern Baptist

inerrantist scholars carefully *qualify* what they mean when they say the Bible is without error. Indeed the word "inerrancy" becomes so heavily guarded and qualified that the final position regarding the text of the Bible is nearly the same for both fundamentalists and moderates.

Inerrantist scholars and leaders admit that "apparent discrepancies, verbal differences, seeming contradictions, and so forth" [54] are in the Bible. But they say these things do not count as "errors," including events recounted out of chronological order, numbers disagreeing, divergent accounts of the same events, passages in one part of the Bible quoted loosely in another part of the Bible. Theologian Kenneth Kantzer referred to "puzzling passages" in the Bible and admitted he has had "a freight-car load of unsolved problems," which, when resolved, led him to "a new freight car." [55]

The Chicago Statement on Biblical Inerrancy, which is being cited with the Baptist Faith and Message by a growing number of current SBC leaders, makes repeated qualifications to its statement on inerrancy. "Scripture is inerrant, not in the sense of being absolutely precise by modern standards, but in the sense of making good its claims and achieving that measure of focused truth at which its authors aimed." [56] However, these inerrantists unanimously agree these "problems" do not count as "errors." In another qualification, the Chicago Statement on Biblical Inerrancy acknowledges "that the authority of Scripture is in no way jeopardized by the fact that the copies we possess are not entirely error-free... no translation is or can be perfect." [57]

Where SBC fundamentalists affirm such qualified views of inerrancy, and some of them do,[58] their hostility toward moderate teachers and preachers is unnecessary. Men like Jerry Vines, copastor of the First Baptist Church, Jacksonville, Florida, and a recent SBC president, say, "I just could not look Southern Baptists in the face and appoint people who believe there are errors in the Bible." [59] And yet their qualifications of the word "inerrant" tacitly admit imperfections in the Bible's text. Still, they continue their vendetta against Southern Baptist scholars whose views do not differ significantly from these inerrantists' views.

Although many takeover leaders have long been aware of how the word "inerrant" is qualified by conservative scholars, they have deceived many sincere rank-and-file Baptist pastors and lay people into believing that their use of the word "inerrant" means exactly what it says: to be without error. One Tennessee pastor who had worked hard in the takeover effort read parts of *The Unfettered Word* by Rob James. The next day he said to James, "You told me some things I didn't know. Some of the people we've looked to as leaders have made some qualifications we didn't know about."[60]

David S. Dockery, now president of Union University in Tennessee, gives six views of inerrancy in his 1991 book, *The Doctrine of the Bible*: naive, absolute, balanced, limited, functional, and errant but authoritative. Dockery admits these views occasionally overlap and different views are held by equally conservative scholars.[61]

(3) Fundamentalists say that most Southern Baptists are inerrantists, but that certain professors are at odds with the people in the pew. Dr.Clark Pinnock, a conservative Baptist who now teaches theology in Canada, makes a convincing argument that moderate Baptists scholars were never far removed from the Biblical theology of the rank-and-file church members.

Pinnock taught at New Orleans Seminary from 1965 until 1969. During that period and after, he was a fiery advocate of roughly the position now held by SBC fundamentalists. He was one of Paige Patterson's favorite seminary professors. Although Pinnock shifted his position on inerrancy in the 1970s,[62] leaders of the nondenominational inerrancy movement still claim him as one of their own.

At the 1987 inerrancy conference, Pinnock said he believed Southern Baptists' typical approach to the Bible is not inerrancy in the strictest sense. Rather, it is what he called "simple biblicism." Simple biblicism, he said, is a view that "most evangelicals and Baptists hold, *whether scholars or not*, because the Spirit teaches it to them." This approach "views the Scriptures as the only place to go if you want to find the words of everlasting life."[63]

At the inerrancy conference, Mark Noll, a distinguished historian at Wheaton College,[64] agreed and explained that in the "Baptist" approach, as he called it, the Bible's truth and authority are known by inward experience, not by rationalistic arguments about the nature of the Bible."[65] This attitude toward the Bible could be called "inerrantist" in a loose, popular sense of the term.[66] But as Pinnock and Noll suggest, moderate Baptist scholars and many lay persons affirmed a "simple Biblicism" that was always sufficient to unify Baptist churches for missions and evangelism. The "inerrancy controversy" was invented to serve as a political weapon.

In any case, it is not difficult to state what unifies Southern Baptists in their approach to the Bible. As Russell Dilday, former president of Southwestern Seminary, the largest SBC seminary, states it, among Southern Baptists "there is practically total unanimity concerning their commitment to the Bible as the divinely inspired, sufficient, certain, and authoritative guide for faith and practice.[67]

If people want to divide the denomination and mobilize one group for conquest over another group, however, the unifying factors we have in common are not the kind of thing these political leaders talk about. Instead, they talk about "inerrancy" and misrepresent the issue.

The air has been turned blue in the SBC with talk of inerrancy. For that reason, "the Bible issue" looms large in the *perceptions* of many people. In that sense, of course, inerrancy has been made an issue. But if one wishes to say where differences lie that are crucial for Southern Baptist denominational life — and that is what inerrantists claim to be talking about — the inerrancy issue is fraudulent.

"Undoubtedly," says Leon McBeth, "history will record that the controversy was not really about the Bible."[68]

11. All About Eve: Kansas City SBC, 1984 Women in Baptist Life

The controversy over the role of women in Southern Baptist life was not new in 1984. Almost a century earlier, in 1885, the SBC constitution was changed to seat "brethren" rather than "messengers" to prevent women being regarded as messengers; women were not accepted as messengers, with full voting privileges, until 1918.[69]

The Watts Street Baptist Church, Durham, North Carolina, ordained the first Southern Baptist woman, Addie Davis, to the ministry in 1964. By 1993, over 1,000 Southern Baptist women would have been ordained, with more than fifty having served as pastors of Southern Baptist churches. Twenty-three women served as senior pastors in 1993. By the end of 1997,[70] an estimated 1,400 women had been ordained (not including deacons). Over 90 women were pastors/co-pastors and approximately 103 were associate pastors.[71]

The 1984 Kansas City Convention, firmly controlled by fundamentalists, resisted this trend and opposed the full equality of women in the church by adopting a strongly worded resolution against ordaining women as deacons or pastors.

WHEREAS, While Paul commends women and men alike in other roles of ministry and service (Titus 2:1-10), he excludes women from pastoral leadership (1 Tim. 2:12) to preserve a submission God requires because the man was first in creation and the woman was first in the Edenic fall (1 Tim 2:13ff); . . .

Therefore, be it *Resolved*, ...we encourage the service of women in all aspects of church life and work other than pastoral functions and leadership roles entailing ordination. [72]

The resolution gave what purports to be the biblical rationale for the hierarchy of men over women in church life: God requires such submission, the resolution argued, because man was first in creation, while woman was first in the Edenic fall.[73]

Some who spoke for the resolution at the time made the point that a resolution does not instruct agencies or churches. It only registers the opinion of those attending that convention. True enough! There was no attempt in 1984 or 1985 to threaten the funding or reshape the policy of agencies that employed ordained women or their husbands. But the groundwork was laid for a later year, when fundamentalists would have majorities on agency and institution boards.[74] (See the next section.)

The 1984 resolution blaming women for the sin in the world (for so it was understood) was greeted with surprise and outrage throughout much of the convention. It helped mobilize many who were just beginning to understand the seriousness of the takeover. A resolution introduced by more moderate messengers at the 1994 SBC in response to the 1984 resolution was not reported out by the resolutions committee because, "the committee saw no reason to alter the Convention's statement of ten years ago." The 1994 resolution stated, in part,

> we remind ourselves of the dearly bought Baptist principle of the final authority of Scripture in matters of faith and conduct, and that we both recognize and encourage the service of women in all aspects of church life and work, including those entailing the tradition of ordination.[75]

What factors led to the 1984 Kansas City resolution? In the broader society, the changing role of women in society played a part in raising expectations of women who professed a religious calling; and these expectations, in turn, heightened the concerns of godly people over the erosion of family life and the increase in divorce and family strife. There were regional differences in theology and practice as well. "East Coast churches have regularly ordained women, while westerners have generally viewed such action as out and out heresy."[76] The growing presence of ordained women, especially in the eastern churches, alarmed church leaders in the deep south and west who demanded a more traditional approach.

In addition, specific actions in several states combined to call attention to the ordination of women as an issue: ordination of three women deacons by First Baptist Church, Oklahoma City, in face of an associational resolution opposing ordination of women; the disfellowshipping of three California churches that ordained women deacons; the calling of a woman as pastor by a church in Chicago; protests in Montana decrying the fact that the Home Mission Board appointed an ordained woman as a church planter; associational actions on women's issues in at least seven states; and Home Mission Board president Bill Tanner's statement that the agency took no position on the ordination of women.[77]

Prior to the 1984 Convention, SBC president James Draper, who had been elected with Pressler-Patterson support, indicated he considered the ordination of women a matter for each church to decide.[78] That view prevailed in December 1984 when the Home Mission Board gave a pastoral assistance grant to a church with a woman pastor in Annapolis, Maryland. The action was upheld by that board's directors in early 1985 by a vote of 39-32. The closeness of the vote suggested what was soon to happen to that board.

In similar fashion the Sunday School Board issued editorial guidelines emphasizing that ordination of deacons and ministers is a matter which falls under the authority of the local church. The Sunday School Board would "continue to affirm and acknowledge the biblical and historic contributions of women to the cause of Christ."[79]

In 1998 BAPTISTS TODAY reprinted a time line of women's role in Southern Baptist life:[80]

1868: Women met during the Southern Baptist Convention and raised $1,299 to support work with women in China.

1885: Women were refused admission to the Southern Baptist Convention annual meeting. The constitution was changed to seat "brethren" rather than "messengers."

1888: Woman's Missionary Union was founded in Richmond, Va., in the basement of a Methodist church because they were not allowed to meet in a Baptist church.

1904: Four women were allowed to attend classes at Southern Seminary. They could not participate in class discussions or take classes for credit.

1918: Women were accepted as messengers to the Southern Baptist Convention annual meeting, with voting privileges. In the same year, the U.S. House of Representatives approved an amendment to the Constitution giving women the right to vote. It was ratified in 1920, 42 years after the amendment was first introduced in Congress.

1929: Mrs. J. W. Cox, WMU president, was the first woman to address the SBC. Previously, men had given the WMU report.

1964: Addie Davis was the first woman ordained to the gospel ministry by a Southern Baptist church, the Watts Street Baptist Church in Durham, N.C.

1980: Anne Rosser, who co-pastored a church in Richmond, Va., with her husband, Aubrey, baptized three new Christians, possibly the first time a woman baptized anyone in Southern Baptist life.

1983: Thirty-three Southern Baptist women met in Louisville, Kentucky for support and encouragement of one another's ministry, and formed Southern Baptist Women in Ministry. The organization dropped "Southern" from its name in July 1995.

1996: Baptist Women in Ministry (BWIM) offices were moved to Central Baptist Theological Seminary in Kansas City, Mo. BWIM publishes a quarterly newsletter, Folio.

12. The First Board Is Taken Over

Adrian Rogers' election as president for a second time in 1986, the eighth straight victory for SBC fundamentalists, signaled a change in the balance of power on the various agency and institution boards. The Home Mission Board (HMB) was the first agency whose board reflected a majority of fundamentalist directors.

Bill Tanner, president of the Home Mission Board, resigned in May 1986 to become executive director of the Baptist General Convention of Oklahoma. In June, the officers of the HMB's board of directors named a 7-person search committee to replace Tanner.

The new fundamentalist majority on the board flexed its muscle by forcing the resignation of the presidential search committee on a 40-36 vote behind closed doors in August 1986. Subsequently, a new search committee nominated Larry L. Lewis, president of Hannibal-LaGrange College, a small Missouri Baptist college. Lewis, a long-time and trusted ally of the takeover coalition, pledged to work with all factions in the SBC after his election in 1987, but moderates saw his election as evidence of fundamentalist control.[81] Lewis served as president of the Home Mission Board until resigning January 1, 1997 to work with parachurch prayer, evangelism and discipleship organization, Mission America.

Once the Home Mission Board was firmly in the hands of the takeover faction, the trustees turned their attention once again to the issue of women's ordination. The Board had addressed this topic in 1985 by approving pastoral assistance and appointing two ordained women to mission ministries. The first was a pastoral assistance grant to Broadneck Baptist church in Annapolis, Maryland, whose pastor was Debra Grittis-Woodberry, the first ordained woman to receive such aid.

The second concerned Janet Fuller, a US-2 missionary assigned as campus minister to Yale University and four other campuses. The Baptist Convention of New England requested that Fuller be appointed a full-time missionary and continue at her post. The HMB personnel committee voted not to appoint her because she was ordained, but HMB directors voted at the October 1985 meeting to appoint her, 37-34. During the same meeting, the directors named a committee to study HMB policy concerning the issue of women's ordination.

A year later, at the October 1986 meeting, the HMB directors adopted new guidelines on the ordination of women. They affirmed a long-standing policy that ordination is not a requirement for missionary service, but they voted not to give future financial support to a church with a woman serving as pastor. The policy on ordination permits the appointment of ordained women as missionaries and the endorsement of ordained women as chaplains, but prohibits future use of HMB funds to support women who serve as pastors of local churches, or local churches who call women as pastors.[82]

Despite SBC president Draper's admonition in 1984 that SBC resolutions do not bind agencies, it was clear that the 1984 resolution on women had worked its way into policy. The fundamentalist faction was quite ready to use its power.

An editorial after the October 1986 decision, in SBC *Today* read:

The message the vote sends to women, while not new, is that they are unwanted and will not be supported as pastors of churches. The message to churches who have ordained or who have called women as pastors is that while their gifts to home missions will be received, their theology is rejected, as are those women who have heard and responded to God's call.[83]

HMB directors, by a vote of 44-24, defeated a motion during the March 1987 meeting to rescind the decision adopted in October to prohibit future financial support of ordained women serving as local church pastors. HMB director Marvin Prude said after the vote, "The HMB is now in the hands of the fundamentalists, and they can do virtually anything they want to within their philosophy."[84] A motion to rescind the 1986 decision was also defeated in August 1990.[85]

Following the implementation of the HMB's new policy regarding pastoral assistance for women, the board also passed formal policies against the appointment or provision of pastoral assistance to missionaries who speak in tongues and missionaries who are divorced. According to the HMB's report in the 1988 Southern Baptist Convention annual, "Divorced persons will not be appointed or approved for missionary service unless the divorce was based on 'Biblical rationale' as outlined by the board. That rationale is defined as being limited to cases of adultery or fornication and in the instance of desertion or physical abandonment by a spouse. Also, no divorced individual will be considered for a pastoral role unless the divorce meets the biblical guidelines and the applicant has not remarried."[86]

13. A Southern Baptist Creed? The 1987 St. Louis SBC

The Southern Baptist Convention at Dallas in 1985 elected a "Peace Committee" of twenty-two persons at the 1985 Dallas Convention. That committee's task was "to determine the sources of the controversy in the denomination, and make findings and recommendations regarding these controversies so that Southern Baptists might effect reconciliation" and continue co-operating.[87]

Moderates and fundamentalists were elected to the committee, as well as persons publicly unaligned. The committee's balance of power, however, was unmistakable. Judging from the results, moderates consistently lost the key votes, though they were usually able to somewhat moderate the results.

The Peace Committee made its report to the St. Louis SBC in 1987. It was adopted by a large majority of the messengers, but the way it came to a vote raises questions about how well informed the messengers could have been regarding the content of the report.

The Peace Committee promised to have its report available weeks before the St. Louis Southern Baptist Convention. The chairman wanted an unanimous vote by members of the committee. Unfortunately, the committee was deadlocked, struggling to negotiate a unanimous agreement, and continued to meet right up through the night before the report was due to be voted on by the convention messengers. Daniel Vestal was unable to attend that meeting, but reports being very dissatisfied with the final report. Further, Vestal says that his service on the Peace Committee was one of the most painful experiences of his ministry, because it became clear to him that the fundamentalist leaders on the committee were not interested in peace so much as they were interested in control of the study's outcome.

The report was released just twelve hours before the scheduled vote. Insufficient copies of the report were printed and thousands of messengers did not see it until the evening session when they voted. Informal surveys suggested that less than a third read the whole report. Consideration of the substance of the report was limited to some ten minutes as efforts to postpone action and to extend the time for discussion were turned back. Shortly after the vote, the appearance of unanimity in the committee evaporated when Winfred Moore, a leading moderate pastor from Texas, resigned from the committee.[88]

The Peace Committee recognized that the controversy in the convention was rooted in both theological and political concerns. The committee recognized the great diversity within Southern Baptist life, but said "this diversity should not create hostility towards each other, stand in the way of genuine cooperation, or interfere with the rights and privileges of all Southern Baptists within the denomination to participate in its affairs."[89]

While diversity is acknowledged in the "recommendations" in the report, the "findings" of the report are presented in a manner suggesting support for a fundamentalist creed rather than an inclusive Baptist confession of faith. In the "findings," the report gives examples of what "most" Southern Baptists think the Baptist Faith and Message means when it says the Bible has "truth without mixture of error for its matter":

(1) They believe in direct creation and therefore they believe Adam and Eve were real persons.

(2) They believe the named authors did indeed write the biblical books attributed to them by those books.

(3) They believe the miracles described in Scripture did indeed occur as supernatural events in history.

(4) They believe that the historical narratives are indeed accurate and reliable as given by those authors.

We call upon Southern Baptist institutions to recognize the great number of Southern Baptists who believe in this interpretation of our confessional statement and, in the future, to build their professional staffs and faculties from those who clearly reflect such dominant convictions and beliefs held by Southern Baptists at large.[90]

These beliefs may or may not represent what "most" Southern Baptists believe. Certainly many moderate Baptists were and still are comfortable with the above listed beliefs. What really separates confessional moderates from creedal fundamentalists is the moderate's tendency to allow fellow Christians greater freedom to differ. Fundamentalists insist that they cannot support or have fellowship with any Christian who disagrees at any point with their list of "commonly held beliefs." In such an atmosphere, "commonly held beliefs" become a creed that members must affirm or else they will not be given a place in the denomination's leadership.

To illustrate, at the North American Mission Board, (formerly the Home Mission Board), these "findings" are used as guidelines for hiring new staff.[91] In June 1988 and October 1990, Home Mission Board president Larry Lewis sent HMB staff copies of the Peace Committee report at the request of the SBC Executive Committee.[92] Retired Sunday School Board president Grady Cothen says the passage quoted above is now the basis for creedal rather than biblical control of the heart of denominational processes.[93] The contrast with the non-creedal roots of the SBC is stark.

14. The Pastor as Pope: 1988 San Antonio SBC

Lay leadership of the church is unbiblical when it weakens the pastor's authority as ruler of the church.... A laity-led, deacon-led church will be a weak church anywhere on God's earth. The pastor is the ruler of the church. There is no other thing than that in the Bible. — W. A. Criswell[94]

The pastor is the ruler of the church.... The pulpit is mine.... The staff is mine and I run that church. — W. A. Criswell[95]

A resolution supporting stronger pastoral authority in the local church, adopted at the 1988 Convention in San Antonio has been one of the most controversial actions of the fundamentalist majority. The resolution was critical of the cardinal Baptist belief in the "priesthood of all believers" or "soul competency."

One of the major foundational ideas of the Protestant Reformation was the teaching that every individual relates directly to God in Christ: No priest stands between the believer and God, and no priest presides over the individual conscience. The believer is solely responsible to God as the Spirit leads him or her.

Originating from the wing of the Reformation that dissented from the state churches, Baptists have been famous for taking this idea more seriously than virtually any other group. The 1963 Baptist Faith and Message reflects this position clearly. A local congregation is self-governing, it says, and "In such a congregation members are equally responsible."[96]

This set of ideas provides the dynamic behind the sometimes bristly democracy one encounters in a Baptist congregation. Every believer is equal before God and other believers. No one is anything but a peer in the Lord — and no one had better try to be anything but a peer! — because each confronts the Lord directly.

Most fundamentalism has a different spirit. Wherever fundamentalists have taken over a Baptist congregation, some parts of the New Testament are suddenly ignored. Other parts are set to new music. The title of the new song is "Pastoral Authority." W. A. Criswell, pastor emeritus of the First Baptist Church, Dallas, told a group of pastors in Tupelo, Mississippi, in 1994, that "The man of God who is the pastor of the church is the ruler."[97] In Criswell's view, the pastor may need no more that a 51 percent majority to be called by a church, but after that, the basic decisions within the church are his to make.

The resolution adopted in San Antonio in 1988, by a vote of 10,950 to 9,050, denigrates the centrality of the priesthood of all believers in Baptist thought: it refers to emphasis on this belief as "a recent historical development" and criticizes the idea of a believer's priesthood as undermining "pastoral authority in the local church."[98]

The 1998 "pastoral authority" resolution presents at least three significant problems to those who seek to be true to our Baptist heritage. First, it rewrites our history — denying the doctrine in the writings of such giants in our denomination as John Smyth, E. Y. Mullins, George W. Truett, Herschel Hobbs, Findley Edge, and others.[99] E. Y. Mullins, principal author of the original Baptist Faith and Message statement in 1925, argued that the "great principle ...[Baptists] contributed to the religious thought and life of mankind" was "the competency of the soul in religion."[100] Other trusted Baptist leaders also affirmed the priesthood of all believers. W. T. Conner, longtime professor of theology at Southwestern Seminary, wrote, "...since the Spirit dwells in all believers, every believer should have the privilege of making known the will of Christ as the Spirit has revealed it to him."[101] *Baptists Ideals*, a document prepared by nineteen Southern Baptist leaders and scholars in 1964, states that the priesthood of believers "means that all members serve as equals under God in the fellowship of a local church."[102] Ironically The San Antonio resolution even ignored the fact that the 1988 doctrinal study book for the Convention was on this particular doctrine!

Second, the resolution creates a hierarchy among believers, setting the "professional ministry" above the lay ministry. This denies the significance of the rending of the veil in the Temple in the passion narratives of the Gospels (see, for example, Luke 23:44-45) as a means of opening access to the altar to all believers and not just the priestly caste. Baptists have long affirmed this. William C. Boone, author of *What We Believe*, wrote in 1936. "There are no rulers within the church. There are no differences among the members in rank or classes. The officers... are elected by vote of all the members, not to rule, but to lead and to serve."[103]

In stark contrast to Boone's affirmation of Christian equality, the action at the San Antonio Convention emphasizes "pastoral authority" in the local church. Such hierarchal concepts of church polity have been foreign and repugnant to Baptist churches and leaders from the very inception of the Baptist movement. As New Testament believers, we regard Jesus Christ as our high priest. All his followers are a part of his priesthood, and the function of the "professional minister" is to equip and enable the laity to be priests and ministers.

Third, the resolution demeans the role of the laity as priests and relieves us of the responsibility to act as priests, seeking God's will and discovering his grace for our own lives.

Most moderates believe the 1988 resolution on the priesthood of all believers represents a grave and dangerous doctrinal assault on what it means to be a Baptist and a Christian. It represents the arrogance of a group that has chosen to exercise its political muscle by, like Esau, selling its birthright of soul freedom for a bowl of the stew of pastoral authority.

While discussions of "soul freedom" and "priesthood of all believers" may seem to be the language of theoretical clergy conflicts, this particular doctrinal revolution of the takeover faction has actually had the most painful impact on the life of the local church. In one congregation after another, where fundamentalist pastors have taken control, the doctrine of pastoral authority has not only preached but lived out by authoritarian ministers, intent dominating most of the church's decisions and actions. Lay leadership has been discounted and intentionally bypassed, while lay members are taught to obey their ministers, because God has placed them "over" the church as spiritual authorities. One example of the practical form this takes can be found at such a heartland congregation as the Second Baptist Church of Hot Springs Arkansas, where people are required to sign a "covenant" as a pre-requisite for membership. In the covenant, among other things they agree to "...protect the unity of Second Baptist Church by following the leaders." As support for this they cite as a prooftext *Hebrews* 13:17, "Obey your leaders and submit to their authority."[104]

At Second Baptist Church in Hot Springs, the ministers are well educated and well intentioned. Their emphasis on obedience to the ministerial leadership is largely kept within the sphere of church affairs. In the hands of lesser men the doctrine can take on an even more dangerous edge, as pastors attempt to interfere in the personal lives of their flock, as if they were indeed sheep rather than people responsible before God for their own decisions. At its best the concept of Pastoral authority leads to benevolent dictatorship. At its most ugly, it leads to the cult of personality, the worship of men in place of God, and the spiritual abuse of congregations.

15. Battle for the Seminaries

Southeastern Seminary

The Southern Baptist seminaries were targeted early on by the takeover faction for close scrutiny, documentation of specific instances of supposed heresy or careless language, and accusations of supposedly liberal leanings. In the first phase of the takeover strategy, the seminaries were the "soft underbelly," the vulnerable institutions targeted for attack in order to sell the rank-and-file on the necessity of returning the SBC to its "conservative moorings."

Paul Pressler, Paige Patterson, and others claimed the seminaries were infiltrated with "liberalism," and that many professors did not believe the Bible. Biblical inerrancy became the issue by which to mobilize the grassroots. "Get rid of the liberals in the seminaries" was the rallying cry to pull people to the annual meeting of the SBC and elect a president who could turn the tide. And it worked.

All the seminaries came under siege. Fundamentalist students were enlisted to spy and report on professors. In 1984 Patterson said the Criswell Center was archiving specific instances of heresy: "Any time these people talk, we have someone there listening and sending us tapes."[105]

Southeastern Seminary professor Alan Neely, now professor of missions at Princeton Theological Seminary, Princeton, New Jersey, was questioned by an SBC watchdog group about statements he supposedly made in class, statements he says he did not make. Neely commented, "It has now become open season on seminary professors.... We have been marginalized and, in many respects, slandered."[106]

By the 1984-85 academic year, the seminary presidents had begun to speak out. Southeastern Seminary president Randall Lolley called the controversy

---

a test to determine whether Southern Baptists will remain a convention of conservative Christians freely cooperating within their local congregations to do evangelism, missions, education, and benevolences or whether they will become a coalition of independent fundamentalists torn asunder by power plays and party spirit.[107]

In October 1986, the six seminary presidents tried with little success to ease the pressure by issuing the so-called "Glorieta Statement." In that statement they agreed to enforce adherence to the seminary's historic doctrinal statements, and expressed their own personal belief that "the sixty-six books of the Bible are not errant in any area of reality." The statement was viewed by some moderates as a capitulation to fundamentalist control, but the presidents insisted it was not.

In the fall of 1987, however, the takeover faction exercised its new majority at Southeastern Seminary with actions further curtailing academic freedom.[108] Faculty members were removed from the selection process for new faculty; the new policy placed responsibility solely with the president who was expected to only nominate faculty who affirmed the Peace Committee report.

In response, Southeastern Seminary president Randall Lolley resigned, as did his academic dean, Morris Ashcraft, and two other aides. They were in an untenable position, they said. The final straw, according to Lolley, was the new board's faculty appointment process. He would not be party to the destruction of "the idea the seminary has sought to incarnate" of free and responsible theological education in a context of free conscience, free church, free country, and free classroom.[109]

Lolley charged that the trustees' pre-packaged agenda led to his resignation. Pre-meeting caucuses by the trustees and pre-arranged maneuverings subverted the process and made his leadership impossible. "Our differences range from matters of governance, through theology and ecclesiology, to management and leadership styles," Lolley said.

Southeastern Seminary professors took steps to protect themselves by organizing a chapter of the American Association of University Professors and by raising money for a legal defense fund. Chapter president Richard Hester affirmed,

---

We will not permit ourselves to be investigated unless formal charges are brought and due process is followed. We will not sign any confessional document [over and above the seminary's historic statement they had already signed] ...and we will operate as a group.[110]

Lolley became pastor of the First Baptist Church in Raleigh, North Carolina, a position that allowed him to be an effective voice for the moderate cause. He was called to the First Baptist Church in Greensboro, North Carolina in 1990.

Lolley's former academic dean, Morris Ashcraft, announced that he would retire at the end of his 1988-89 sabbatical leave. During that year, he was active in negotiations, under the auspices of the Southern Baptist Alliance, aimed at the creation of a new seminary which would carry on the dream of Southeastern. The decision to open such a seminary in Richmond, Virginia, would be made in October 1988.[111]

Lewis A. Drummond, previously Billy Graham Professor of Evangelism at Southern Seminary, was installed as the fourth president at Southeastern Seminary in October 1988. The following March, L. Russ Bush III, associate professor of philosophy of religion at Southwestern Seminary, was elected academic vice-president and dean of the faculty, despite unanimous faculty opposition. Bush circulated a memo prior to his election, stating, "It is absolutely essential that a conservative majority on the faculty be achieved as soon as possible."[112]

In response to these developments, the Association of Theological Schools (ATS) in the U.S. and Canada told Southeastern in June 1989 to "show cause ...why it should not be placed on probation."[113] In December 1989, the Southern Association of Colleges and Schools (SACS), another regional accreditation agency, gave Southeastern Seminary two years to resolve problems brought to light after Lolley's resignation, or be placed on probation.[114] During those two years, the seminary was given a "warning," the second of three levels of sanction.[115] When the seminary failed to correct problems of long-range planning and trustee involvement in selection of faculty, SACS placed the seminary on probation in December 1991. Student enrollment had fallen from 1,098 in 1987 to 603 in 1991.[116] Enrollment has since begun to recover. SACS reaffirmed Southeastern accreditation in December 1993.

In 1991, Southeastern Seminary became the first SBC seminary to include an explicit commitment to biblical inerrancy in its new statement of purpose.[117]

After months of speculation, seminary president Drummond announced his retirement in January 1992, to be effective June 30. Trustees rejected Drummond's request to be named chancellor and to be given a seven-month sabbatical.[118] Drummond was later named Billy Graham Professor of Evangelism and Church Growth at Samford's Beeson Divinity School. Paige Patterson, president of Criswell College in Dallas and one of the chief architects of the takeover, was elected Southeastern Seminary president in May 1992.[119]

Within two weeks of taking office as president in July 1992, Patterson announced that a second accrediting agency, the Association of Theological Schools, had placed the seminary on probation for two years.[120] The seminary's accreditation was reaffirmed by the ATS in June 1994.[121] Within two months of taking office, Patterson announced seven new faculty members for the seminary, six from Criswell College, a fundamentalist Bible school founded through the First Baptist Church of Dallas.[122] They replaced seminary professors who resigned or retired in the face of the fundamentalist takeover. Fundamentalists regarded this swift gain of new ground as a "miracle." In 1994, seminary trustees voted to establish a chair of evangelism in honor of evangelist Bailey Smith, a major leader of the takeover movement, who served as SBC president in 1980-1982.[123]

Southern Seminary

Fundamentalists gained voting majority on the Southern Seminary board of trustees in April 1990. The new majority began implementing the takeover faction's agenda immediately. The trustees granted permission for students to use tape recorders in all seminary classrooms. Prior to this vote, this decision had been left to each professor. The taping of classes was used by some students to record departures from traditional doctrine. Some professors saw this as an implicit threat to their academic freedom.

The trustees also went into a four-hour closed-door session to discuss charges brought by trustee Jerry Johnson of Colorado.

Johnson accused seminary President Roy Honeycutt and several faculty of "doctrinal infidelity," along with other charges. The charges, outlined in a 16-page diatribe titled "The Cover-Up at Southern Seminary," were published in a report about the meeting by The Southern Baptist Advocate, a fundamentalist publication. After considerable discussion, the trustees approved Johnson's request to "postpone indefinitely" his own motion.[124] In response to Johnson's charge that he did not believe the Bible, Honeycutt responded, "You can tell me you disagree with my interpretation of Scripture, but please don't tell me you disagree with my belief in the Bible."[125]

Facing an untenable relationship with a hostile board of trustees, president Honeycutt opted for retirement at the end of 1993, three years before he had hoped to retire. Albert Mohler, 33, editor of Georgia Baptists' The Christian Index and described as "a hero of SBC fundamentalists," was elected president of Southern Seminary in 1993 to succeed the retiring Honeycutt.[126]

Also in March 1993 seminary trustees, without explanation, refused to approve appointments to endowed chairs for three professors: Gerald Keown, Raymond Bailey, and William Hendricks. Rumor circulated that the refusal stemmed from the professors' memberships in churches which allow members to channel money to Cooperative Baptist Fellowship.[127] Keown was eventually named to an endowed chair in October 1993; the other two professors were never given their expected appointments.

Southern Seminary announced in early 1994 that it would no longer set up exhibits or sponsor gatherings at CBF or CBF-related meetings. The ban applies only to CBF, not to other non-SBC groups or organizations.[128] Other seminaries adopted similar bans.

In September 1994, Mohler forced popular associate professor of theology Molly Marshall to resign her position. Marshall was the first woman granted tenure in the seminary's school of theology. Mohler said he had "significant concerns" about Marshall's adherence to the seminary's Abstract of Principles. Only half-joking, Southern Seminary professor William Hendricks said Marshall's only apparent "crime" was "being born a threateningly brilliant woman." Mohler denied Marshall's gender was a factor in her forced resignation.[129] Marshall accepted a faculty position with Central Baptist Theological Seminary, affiliated with American Baptist Churches, in August 1995.

On March 20, 1995, Mohler fired Diana Garland from her position as Dean of Carver School of Social Work at the seminary. Garland told a student forum the future of the Carver School was "in serious jeopardy" after Mohler blocked the election of a professor for Carver because that candidate said it might be possible for God to call a woman to be a pastor. Removed as Dean, Garland still remained on the seminary faculty. At their next meeting, seminary trustees affirmed Mohler and granted him more authority over faculty. Mohler said future faculty must oppose women serving as pastors.[130] Garland accepted a position with Louisville Presbyterian Seminary, and in 1996 she and husband David accepted faculty positions at Baylor University in Waco, Texas.

Southern Seminary transferred the Carver School of Church Social Work to Campbellsville University in Kentucky in 1997. Seminary trustees said the school was incompatible with the seminary's new direction. A seminary spokesman said a $1 million endowment originally given to the seminary by Woman's Missionary Union to the Carver School would not be given to Campbellsville University.[131]

In a more recent event, Paul Debusman, reference librarian at Southern Seminary, was 10 months away from retirement after serving the seminary for 35 years when seminary president Al Mohler gave him one month's severance pay and fired him in September 1997. Debusman had written SBC president Tom Eliff a private letter to correct what he perceived as historical inaccuracies in Eliff's chapel address. Eliff had said in his address "that in former days he would not have been invited" to speak in chapel at the seminary. Debusman reminded Eliff that in the past "we had heard SBC presidents and other ranking members of the Southern Baptist Convention," including such fundamentalist leaders as W. A. Criswell of the First Baptist Church of Dallas. That letter was the catalyst in Debusman being fired.[132]

In 1991, during Dr. Honeycutt's tenure, Southern Seminary administration, faculty and trustees signed a "Covenant Renewal" document agreeing to bring theological balance to the faculty by adding more "conservative evangelical" scholars to the faculty. Within a turnover of more than 70 percent, Julian Pentecost, a former trustee from Virginia and chair of the committee that drafted the Covenant Renewal document, citing a faculty turnover of 70 percent by 1998, said the makeup of the faculty "has gone far beyond the point of balance." In response, Mohler said, "I think there are many different interpretations of what that balance would look like." He added that the document was "a bridge instrument... to find a way through an impasse."[133]

Forty-two full-time Southern Seminary faculty members resigned, retired or were fired between the fall of 1992, when Roy Honeycutt announced plans to retire as president, and June 1996. Three academic departments experienced a complete turnover or loss of faculty.[134]

Southwestern Seminary

We don't need a reason. We can do it. We have the votes, and we will [fire Dilday]. – Trustee chair Ralph Pulley to Russell Dilday before the trustees voted to fire him.

The premier achievement of the takeover faction at Southwestern Baptist Theological Seminary was the dismissal of seminary president Russell H. Dilday. Dr. Dilday was one of the most popular agency or institution heads Southern Baptists ever had. Named president at Southwestern (SWBTS) in 1977, Dilday considered himself a thoroughgoing theological conservative, but he objected to the harsh spirit and the assault on Baptist freedoms associated with the takeover faction. As a result, he became a target as the fundamentalist uprising gained speed in the mid-1980s.

Dilday and SWBTS trustees reached a compromise over his role in the denominational controversy during a six-hour closed door session in October 1989. Ken Lilly, a trustee from Arkansas who had mailed 86 pages of press clippings which he claimed were "political" statements by Dilday, said after the meeting, that Dilday was "one of the premier leaders in the SBC," and that "Dilday is free to speak his conscience."[135] A few months later, in early 1990, *Christianity Today*, named Southwestern Seminary the top theological seminary in the United States.[136]

While at the 1990 SBC in New Orleans, Dilday was quoted as saying the "crass, secular political methodology used in the take-over of the convention these past 12 years has satanic and evil qualities to which I am desperately opposed." Seminary trustee chair Jimmy Draper was reported to have called other trustees about a possible meeting to "deal with Dilday." Dilday explained he was not implying that fellow believers were satanic.[137]

Trustees lauded Dilday for 15 years of "able leadership and administration" of the seminary during his March 1993 evaluation.[138] He was then abruptly fired March 9, 1994, only one day after he had received the favorable job-performance evaluation and trustees said no action was planned against the embattled president. Trustees gave no official reasons for the firing. Trustee chair Ralph Pulley, a member of First Baptist Church in Dallas, told Dilday, "We don't need a reason. We can do it. We have the votes, and we will."[139] Pulley was a trustee in 1977 and voted against Dilday when he was elected president; some have accused Pulley of leading a personal vendetta against Dilday.[140]

Trustees voted on preprinted ballots. Two letters were also pre-prepared; one if Dilday retired and the other if he were fired. Some faculty members received the wrong letter. Within minutes of the firing, trustees changed locks of the president's office and denied him access. John Earl Seelig, a former seminary vice president, was placed in charge of the seminary's public relations. Seelig said he had been asked to take the position prior to the firing.[141]

During the same meeting, trustees withdrew a 3-year-old invitation extended to Keith Parks, extended while he was still president of the Foreign Mission Board, to speak at the seminary's upcoming spring commencement. William B. Tolar, vice president for academic affairs and provost of the seminary since 1990 and a faculty member since 1965, was later named acting president of the seminary.

In response to widespread anger across the SBC, seminary trustees mailed 40,000 letters to pastors and directors of missions at a cost of $11,000 to explain their reasons for firing Dilday.[142] In addition to failing to support the takeover, The letter accused Dilday of holding "liberal views of scripture."[143] The letter specifically accused Dilday of demonstrating "a commitment to the principles of higher criticism, which spawned theological liberalism (modernism), neo-orthodoxy, the death of God, situational ethics, etc." Dilday said he was "appalled" by the "inaccuracies and distortions of truth" in the trustees' letter.[144] Seminary faculty, in an open letter to Southern Baptists, rejected the charges in the trustees' letter and affirmed Dilday for his conservative theology and "traditional, conservative Southern Baptist views of the Scriptures."[145]

In 1994, the Association of Theological Schools (ATS), one of SWBTS's accrediting agencies, cited six concerns regarding Dilday's firing and called for the seminary to show cause why it should not be placed on probation. ATS executive director James Waits said the firing was "a clear violation of acceptable governance practices"[146] and issued a written rebuke to the trustees. In early 199,[147] ATS placed Southwestern Seminary on probation for two years.

Among its findings, ATS said a survey of the faculty found 67.2 percent of the faculty said academic freedom of some professors had been violated, and 88.1 percent said trustees were not acting responsibly in guiding the seminary.[148] The probation was lifted early in June 1996.

In July 1994, seminary trustees unanimously elected church growth strategist and former pastor, Kenneth S. Hemphill, 46, as the 7th president of the seminary. Hemphill said he was dedicated to hiring faculty who were committed to biblical inerrancy.[149] At about the same time, Dilday announced he would join Baylor University's new George W. Truett Theological Seminary as distinguished professor of homiletics and special assistant to the university's president, effective August 1, 1994.[150]

Other SBC Seminaries

Female pastors "is one of the raging, raging heresies and confusions of the day, and it's just eating up churches." — Mark Coppenger[151]

Golden Gate Seminary president Frank Pollard resigned in 1986 to return to First Baptist Church, Jackson, Mississippi as pastor. William Crews was elected his successor.

Midwestern Seminary trustees denied tenure to theology professor Wilburn Stancil in April 1993.[152] Trustees voted to deny tenure to Stancil again in October 1993. Stancil said he accepted the verbal inspiration of the Bible, but trustees denied him tenure because he would not avow inerrancy.[153] Stancil's teaching contract at Midwestern Seminary expired in June 1994.

Milton Ferguson, president of Midwestern Baptist Theological Seminary since 1973, announced in April 1994 that he would retire at the end of July 1996.

After serving as executive-director-treasurer of the State Convention of Baptists in Indiana, Mark Coppenger, SBC Executive Committee vice-president since 1991 was elected president of Midwestern Seminary in a special called meeting in June 1995.[154]

Coppenger soon drew a response from the seminary's Virginia state alumni chapter for saying that Midwestern is "a seminary waiting to happen" and that a "prairie fire" needs to burn at Midwestern and it needs to "burn off the clutter." The chapter, in a open letter published in the Religious Herald, the state Baptist paper in Virginia, said the seminary has been "happening" in very positive ways for decades and wondered if hundreds of alumni were being categorized as "clutter."[155]

In September 1994, Vernon Davis, vice president for academic affairs and dean of the faculty at Midwestern Seminary, resigned to become dean of the new Logsdon School of Theology at Hardin-Simmons University in Abilene, Texas. In 1998, Midwestern Seminary trustees approved changes to the seminary's purpose statement affirming the Bible is the "inerrant" word of God and saying that women are not to serve as pastors. Women are still allowed in the degree track most often taken by pastors, but "alternative courses are now prescribed for women to take instead of the normal courses in preaching and pastoral leadership."[156]

Landrum P. Leavell II, president of New Orleans Baptist Theological Seminary since 1974, also announced in April 1994 that he would retire by the end of 1996. He announced he would become chancellor at some point prior to that date to assist the seminary in fund-raising. However, in December 1994, Leavell surprised seminary trustees with his announcement that he would retire at the end of the month.[157] Chuck Kelley, professor of evangelism at New Orleans Seminary since 1983, was elected president of the school effective March 1, 1996. Kelley's sister, Dorothy, is the wife of Paige Patterson, president of Southeastern Seminary.[158]

In 1997, New Orleans Seminary withdrew invitations to two pastors to serve as adjunct instructors for the seminary. The invitations were withdrawn because the two men had connections with the Cooperative Baptist Fellowship. Jon Stubblefield, pastor of First Baptist Church, Shreveport, La., was approached about teaching Greek at the seminary's Shreveport extension center. The seminary first told Stubblefield the course had been canceled for financial reasons. When Stubblefield said he would teach the course for free, he was told he was disqualified because he had spoken at a state CBF meeting. This was done despite obvious loyalty to the SBC on the part of Stubblefield's church. His church gave $65,000 to the Lottie Moon offering in 1996 and $20,000 to the Annie Armstrong offering in 1997. Most denominational communities would surely consider such support a cause for gratitude. Philip Wise, pastor of First Baptist Church, Dothan, Ala., was assured "politics" were not a factor in selecting faculty for off-campus courses when he was "talked into" teaching a two-term course at the seminary's Alabama center. Near the end of the first term, Wise was told he could not be used in the second term because of his "connection" with CBF.[159]

16. Calvinism Promoted by New SBC Leaders

Sit down, young man. When God decides to save the heathen, he will do it without your help or mine! — Calvinist Baptist to William Carey[160]

Another development that has alarmed mission-minded moderates has been the growing influence of the theology known as Calvinism, among some fundamentalist leaders. To simplify a very complex matter, Calvinism teaches that God has already predestined every eternal soul to heaven or hell, and human freedom to choose plays no part in this decision. It is obvious that this view would create problems for the theological foundation and personal motivation to support missions and evangelism.

While Calvinism has gained many adherents in the fundamentalist community, there are still many fundamentalists who do not subscribe at all to that philosophy. Paige Patterson, President of Southeastern Seminary, Adrian Rogers, Pastor of Bellevue Baptist Church and Richard Land, Director of the SBC Ethics and Religious Liberty Commission, all passionately oppose Calvinism. There are, however, some prominent fundamentalist leaders who have embraced the concept.

Calvinism takes its name from Reformed theologian John Calvin (1509-1564). Five-point Calvinism, advocated by Southern Baptist Calvinists such as Mark Coppenger, Al Mohler, and Tom Nettles was adopted by the Synod of Dort in 1618-19 in the Netherlands. Perhaps the doctrine is appealing to some fundamentalists because it is utterly systematic rather than personal, exclusionary in the extreme and calls for a literal interpretation

bers of the board of regents. The board of trustees was eliminated; authority to govern Baylor rests solely within the board of regents. Baylor received $6 million of its 1990 $102 million budget from the BGCT.

Baylor University incorporated the George W. Truett Theological Seminary in 1991. It welcomed its first students in the fall of 1994. Regents also approved a plan to operate satellites in three Texas cities if needed.[169] Russell Dilday was named interim dean in March 1995 after seminary dean Robert Sloan was elected president of Baylor University.

Also in October 1990, trustees of Furman University in Greenville, South Carolina, voted to elect their own trustees. University president John Johns said the action was taken "to move our governing body out of harm's way, so it can go back to an emphasis on education, rather than being a pawn in the political field."[170] In an agreement with the state convention, the convention will select trustees from a list submitted by the university. Furman receives about three percent of its budget from the South Carolina Baptist Convention.

Samford University in Birmingham, Alabama, received $38.8 million from the late Ralph W. Beeson in 1990. Part of the gift was used for the new Beeson Divinity School, which Beeson's will said "must remain independent from Baptist doctrine."[171]

In September 1994, Samford trustees voted to elect their own successors, in effect loosening the historic ties with the Alabama Baptist Convention.

Two weeks after the Samford action, Mississippi College trustees announced that in an effort to shield the college from the fundamentalist controversy, they would also elect their own successors. However, the college, after negotiations with the state convention, agreed that future trustees would be elected by the state convention after approval by college trustees.[172]

Carson-Newman College trustees voted in April 1998 to change their trustee selection process and return the 147-year-old Jefferson City, Tenn., institution to its original method of naming

---

of certain Biblical texts, without consideration for how the rest of the Bible's message might effect the interpretation of those texts. Fundamentalists tend to share that affinity for systematic, impersonal theology, exclusionary fellowship and simplistic Biblical literalism.

Classic Calvinism rests on the foundation of five propositions. Those "five points" are often referred to using the acronym TULIP.[161]

T   Total depravity of human nature.

U   Unconditional election, in that humans are not chosen for salvation on the basis of any foreseen merit, quality, or achievement.

L   Limited atonement, in that Christ died only for the elect, or those chosen by God. Not all humans have been chosen for salvation; those not chosen are destined for eternal punishment from before birth.

I   Irresistible grace; those chosen for salvation cannot refuse to receive it. It is irresistible.

P   Perseverance of the saints, in that those chosen for salvation cannot lose it.

A gathering of seven persons in Euless, Texas in November 1982 was the beginning of an effort to turn the Southern Baptist Convention toward a more strict Calvinist doctrine. Early Southern Baptist leaders were influenced to a certain extent by Calvinism, but generally rejected the Calvinist teaching of "limited atonement." Limited Atonement is the position that God elects certain persons for salvation and others for damnation. No matter how much a person may want to repent, Calvinists say, only God's elect are able to repent and believe.

Calvinist Timothy George of Beeson Divinity School in Birmingham, Alabama, says, "Whosoever will believe may be saved. But it is efficient only among those whom God has elected to salvation." Outspoken Calvinist Al Mohler, president of Southern Seminary, says believing that God alone determines who will be saved also requires a belief that God has chosen some people not to be saved.[162]

William R. Estep, distinguished professor of church history emeritus at Southwestern Seminary, said in 1997, "Baptists have never been doctrinaire Calvinists, as a careful study of the sources (reveals)." Estep said, "Most of the ardent advocates of this movement have only a slight knowledge of Calvin or his system."[163]

Despite alarm from moderates and fellow fundamentalists, Calvinism continues to make inroads into Southern Baptist institutions. In 1997, Tom Nettles, an ardent defender of five-point Calvinism, joined the Southern Seminary faculty.

Fisher Humphreys, professor of religion at Samford University's Beeson Divinity School said Calvinists and non-Calvinists have been a part of the SBC since its founding, but over time the SBC has moved away from Calvinism, affirming freedom of the human will to choose Christ as personal savior and Lord. This doctrinal direction has been important to our drive for evangelism and missions.[164]

17. Falwell Endorses "Fundamentalist" Seminaries

The current SBC leadership have generally rejected the term "fundamentalist," preferring to call themselves "conservatives." It is therefore revealing to note that fundamentalists who embrace that term as a proud badge of true belief, also embrace the takeover faction's leadership within the SBC as truly kindred spirits. For many years Independent Baptists refused to align with the SBC because they saw it as "too liberal." Undisputed fundamentalist leaders no longer see the SBC in that way.

Jerry Falwell is the fundamentalist pastor of Thomas Road Baptist Church, and founder of Liberty University in Virginia and the defunct Moral Majority. In the July 1998 issue of his *National Liberty Journal* newspaper, he gives a glowing endorsement of the

SBC, its seminaries and agencies. "All six SBC semir have fundamentalist presidents and faculties," he wr its agencies now have fundamentalist leadership. The o ing majority of its pastors are Bible-believing men of G

Falwell predicted that more independent fundamentalis churches will follow his lead and join the SBC, saying, our sister churches have done the same [joined the S many more will in the months and years to come."[165]

18. Southern Ba[ ] and [ ]

While the six Southern Baptist seminaries are owned and ated by the Southern Baptist Convention, Baptist college universities are not directly affiliated with the national de nation. Trustees of the Southern Baptist colleges and uni ties are elected by the various state conventions which co ute to the support of the schools. Trustees of several sch have taken action to prevent a fundamentalist takeover of institutions by severing relationships with their state con tions.

Wake Forest University severed formal ties to the North Caro Baptist Convention in 1986 after a 52-year relationship. In 19 the university trustees approved creation of a divinity sch when adequate funding is secured.[166] The university receive $293,713 grant in 1994 to help open a divinity school.[167]

Stetson University in Florida worked out an agreement in 19 to gradually severe their relationship with the Florida Bapti Convention. All state convention support ended in 1995.

Baylor University's formation of a board of regents in Octobe 1990 to free the Waco, Texas school from perceived threats of a fundamentalist takeover, has created the greatest outcry from fundamentalists. Jimmy Draper called the Baylor charter change "a modern-day act of piracy."[167] The Baptist General Conven- tion of Texas (BGCT) will elect twenty-five percent of the mem-

of certain Biblical texts, without consideration for how the rest of the Bible's message might effect the interpretation of those texts. Fundamentalists tend to share that affinity for systematic, impersonal theology, exclusionary fellowship and simplistic Biblical literalism.

Classic Calvinism rests on the foundation of five propositions. Those "five points" are often referred to using the acronym TULIP.[161]

T   Total depravity of human nature.

U   Unconditional election, in that humans are not chosen for salvation on the basis of any foreseen merit, quality, or achievement.

L   Limited atonement, in that Christ died only for the elect, or those chosen by God. Not all humans have been chosen for salvation; those not chosen are destined for eternal punishment from before birth.

I   Irresistible grace; those chosen for salvation cannot refuse to receive it. It is irresistible.

P   Perseverance of the saints, in that those chosen for salvation cannot lose it.

A gathering of seven persons in Euless, Texas in November 1982 was the beginning of an effort to turn the Southern Baptist Convention toward a more strict Calvinist doctrine. Early Southern Baptist leaders were influenced to a certain extent by Calvinism, but generally rejected the Calvinist teaching of "limited atonement." Limited Atonement is the position that God elects certain persons for salvation and others for damnation. No matter how much a person may want to repent, Calvinists say, only God's elect are able to repent and believe.

Calvinist Timothy George of Beeson Divinity School in Birmingham, Alabama, says, "Whosoever will believe may be saved. But it is efficient only among those whom God has elected to salvation." Outspoken Calvinist Al Mohler, president of Southern Seminary, says believing that God alone determines who will be saved also requires a belief that God has chosen some people not to be saved.[162]

William R. Estep, distinguished professor of church history emeritus at Southwestern Seminary, said in 1997, "Baptists have never been doctrinaire Calvinists, as a careful study of the sources (reveals)." Estep said, "Most of the ardent advocates of this movement have only a slight knowledge of Calvin or his system."[163]

Despite alarm from moderates and fellow fundamentalists, Calvinism continues to make inroads into Southern Baptist institutions. In 1997, Tom Nettles, an ardent defender of five-point Calvinism, joined the Southern Seminary faculty.

Fisher Humphreys, professor of religion at Samford University's Beeson Divinity School said Calvinists and non-Calvinists have been a part of the SBC since its founding, but over time the SBC has moved away from Calvinism, affirming freedom of the human will to choose Christ as personal savior and Lord. This doctrinal direction has been important to our drive for evangelism and missions.[164]

17. Falwell Endorses "Fundamentalist" Seminaries

The current SBC leadership have generally rejected the term "fundamentalist," preferring to call themselves "conservatives." It is therefore revealing to note that fundamentalists who embrace that term as a proud badge of true belief, also embrace the takeover faction's leadership within the SBC as truly kindred spirits. For many years Independent Baptists refused to align with the SBC because they saw it as "too liberal." Undisputed fundamentalist leaders no longer see the SBC in that way.

Jerry Falwell is the fundamentalist pastor of Thomas Road Baptist Church, and founder of Liberty University in Virginia and the defunct Moral Majority. In the July 1998 issue of his *National Liberty Journal* newspaper, he gives a glowing endorsement of the

SBC, its seminaries and agencies. "All six SBC seminaries now have fundamentalist presidents and faculties," he wrote. "All of its agencies now have fundamentalist leadership. The overwhelming majority of its pastors are Bible-believing men of God."

Falwell predicted that more independent fundamentalist Baptist churches will follow his lead and join the SBC, saying, "Many of our sister churches have done the same [joined the SBC] and many more will in the months and years to come."[165]

18. Southern Baptist Colleges and Universities

While the six Southern Baptist seminaries are owned and operated by the Southern Baptist Convention, Baptist colleges and universities are not directly affiliated with the national denomination. Trustees of the Southern Baptist colleges and universities are elected by the various state conventions which contribute to the support of the schools. Trustees of several schools have taken action to prevent a fundamentalist takeover of their institutions by severing relationships with their state conventions.

Wake Forest University severed formal ties to the North Carolina Baptist Convention in 1986 after a 52-year relationship. In 1989, the university trustees approved creation of a divinity school when adequate funding is secured.[166] The university received a $293,713 grant in 1994 to help open a divinity school.[167]

Stetson University in Florida worked out an agreement in 1990 to gradually sever their relationship with the Florida Baptist Convention. All state convention support ended in 1995.

Baylor University's formation of a board of regents in October 1990 to free the Waco, Texas school from perceived threats of a fundamentalist takeover, has created the greatest outcry from fundamentalists. Jimmy Draper called the Baylor charter change "a modern-day act of piracy."[167] The Baptist General Convention of Texas (BGCT) will elect twenty-five percent of the members of the board of regents. The board of trustees was eliminated; authority to govern Baylor rests solely within the board of regents. Baylor received $6 million of its 1990 $102 million budget from the BGCT.

Baylor University incorporated the George W. Truett Theological Seminary in 1991. It welcomed its first students in the fall of 1994. Regents also approved a plan to operate satellites in three Texas cities if needed.[169] Russell Dilday was named interim dean in March 1995 after seminary dean Robert Sloan was elected president of Baylor University.

Also in October 1990, trustees of Furman University in Greenville, South Carolina, voted to elect their own trustees. University president John Johns said the action was taken "to move our governing body out of harm's way, so it can go back to an emphasis on education, rather than being a pawn in the political field."[170] In an agreement with the state convention, the convention will select trustees from a list submitted by the university. Furman receives about three percent of its budget from the South Carolina Baptist Convention.

Samford University in Birmingham, Alabama, received $38.8 million from the late Ralph W. Beeson in 1990. Part of the gift was used for the new Beeson Divinity School, which Beeson's will said "must remain independent from Baptist doctrine."[171]

In September 1994, Samford trustees voted to elect their own successors, in effect loosening the historic ties with the Alabama Baptist Convention.

Two weeks after the Samford action, Mississippi College trustees announced that in an effort to shield the college from the fundamentalist controversy, they would also elect their own successors. However, the college, after negotiations with the state convention, agreed that future trustees would be elected by the state convention after approval by college trustees.[172]

Carson-Newman College trustees voted in April 1998 to change their trustee selection process and return the 147-year-old Jefferson City, Tenn., institution to its original method of naming

trustees. In the future, trustees will select their own successors, all of whom must be Baptist.[173]

In 1992, Gardner-Webb College in Boiling Springs, North Carolina, announced plans to establish a new school of divinity.[174]

Hardin-Simmons University in Abilene, Texas, offered a master of divinity degree through its Lodsdon School of Theology beginning in 1995.[175]

In June 1994, Mercer University in Macon, Georgia approved a school of theology in Atlanta, with an opening date of fall 1996. A campaign was launched to raise a minimum $5 million endowment plus annual operating expenses.[176] The Mercer School of Theology was renamed the James and Carolyn McAfee School of Theology after the McAfees gave a $10 million endowment gift to the theology school.[177] Alan Culpepper, professor of New Testament at Baylor University, was named the first dean.

Baptists in Northern Virginia opened the John Leland Center for Theological Studies in Falls Church, a Washington, D.C. suburb, with classes to begin in late 1998 or early 1999. Columbia Baptist Church will host the Leland Center, with additional early support from two associations, the D.C. Baptist Convention and the Baptist General Association of Virginia.[178]

Campbellsville University in Kentucky announced it will offer a master of arts degree in Christian studies beginning in the fall of 1998.[179] The new Baptist Seminary of Kentucky in Georgetown hopes to accept its first students in the fall of 1999. It will be owned by its own self-perpetuating board of directors.[180]

Other non-SBC-related schools have begun programs to attract Baptist students: the Baptist Studies Program at Duke Divinity School in Durham, North Carolina in 1990, the House of Baptist Studies at Emory University in Atlanta in 1991, and the Baptist Studies Program at Texas Christian University in Ft. Worth.

19. Church and State: Baptist Joint Committee Under Siege

One of the early objectives of fundamentalists was to withdraw support from, or replace, the staff and leadership of the Baptist Joint Committee on Public Affairs (BJC) in Washington, D.C. That committee represented most of the Baptist denominations in America. In 1988-89, approximately 60 percent of its financial support came from the SBC.[181]

The traditional role of the Baptist Joint Committee has been to serve as a voice for Baptists in this country regarding issues impinging on religious liberty. The committee has generally rejected efforts to use its influence outside the focus on religious liberty issues... Instead, the BJC has sought to be an effective voice in favor of maintaining the separation of church and state. This has been particularly true under the dynamic leadership of its long-time director, retiring in 1999, James Dunn, himself a Southern Baptist minister.

As fundamentalists consolidated their power within the SBC and its agencies and institutions, they began to look longingly at the BJC as a vehicle for advancing the fundamentalist political agenda of those directing the takeover. (More on this in a later section.)

Over several decades, the BJC had painstakingly established credibility at the national level by avoiding extraneous political causes, and by consistently speaking out for religious liberty, while refusing to identify with any political party. The takeover leaders saw its prestige as an important political tool. Thus, through the Southern Baptist appointments to the BJC's trustees and through the leverage generated by the SBC's financial support, leaders of the takeover sought to use the BJC as a mouthpiece on issues such as abortion, school prayer, federal aid to parochial schools and other issues on the agenda of the religious right. When the BJC resisted these efforts, a movement was begun to defund the BJC and to use the funds for the Southern Baptist Public Affairs Committee (PAC).

Many Southern Baptists objected to the PAC's outright partisan actions, not because they disagreed necessarily with the political judgments (they may personally have agreed with those judgments), but because the PAC was breaking precedents of long standing by involving the SBC in highly partisan issues. There were objections when the PAC urged the president to veto a piece of civil rights legislation. The largest outcry came when the PAC endorsed Robert Bork to the U.S. Supreme Court. For most of its history, the SBC had avoided partisan endorsement of political parties and candidates out of deference to the fact that within the convention, honest and well-informed people might arrive at different political opinions. The fundamentalist leadership in the convention was no longer content to extend that traditional courtesy.

In an anguished open letter, the late Porter Routh, who had served longest as Executive Secretary of the Southern Baptist Executive Committee, cited numerous bylaws that were violated by the PAC, as well as precedents reaching back to the Al Smith U.S. presidential candidacy in 1928. He wrote,

> The issue is not the approval of a particular candidate for a position on the Supreme Court... The issue is that the SBC has never and should not now, as a convention, be urging the election of any candidate for any office.[182]

The SBC Executive Committee voted in 1989 to recommend that the convention create its own Religious Liberty Commission to bypass the BJC. When messengers at the June 1989 SBC voiced strong opposition to a new commission, the Executive Committee voted to delay the recommendation and then dropped the idea at their September 1989 meeting. The SBC Christian Life Commission was, instead, given significant new assignments in church-state relations to circumvent the BJC.[183] Meanwhile, the 1989 SBC messengers reduced 1990 SBC support to $400,000 for the BJC. SBC support of the BJC declined as follows:

1989	$448,400
1990	$400,000
1991	$391,796
1992	$50,000
1993	0

The loss of Southern Baptist support of the BJC was made up for by several state conventions, the Cooperative Baptist Fellowship and numerous individuals, while official SBC representation for public affairs was assumed by the Christian Life Commission, which expanded its office in Washington, D.C. In late 1998, the BJC successfully completed a $600,000 endowment drive to ensure its future as a voice for religious liberty in Washington, D.C.

20. A New Moral/Political Agenda

The go-along, get-along strategy is dead. No more engagement. We want a wedding ring, we want a ceremony, we want a consummation of the marriage. — Richard Land, president of the Ethics and Religious Liberty Commission (formerly Christian Life Commission) to the Republican Party[184]

The Christian Life Commission (CLC) is the SBC agency responsible for recommending the SBC's position on moral and ethic issues, and for providing information and programs of action in these matters. (By contrast, the Baptist Joint Committee represents several Baptist bodies, and has limited itself to issues involving religious liberty and the separation of church and state.)

In 1986, Foy Valentine, long-time director of the Christian Life Commission, was approaching retirement. As a result, the agency became a target for fundamentalist control. The agency furnishes an excellent example of how the takeover strategy operates, and what its results are.

By the beginning of 1987, the Commission's Board of Trustees had a majority of takeover members, with more scheduled to be appointed at its next session. At a called meeting on January 15, 1987, Foy Valentine resigned and was given "developmental responsibilities" to tide him over until his impending retirement. Larry Baker, an ethicist serving as vice-president for Academic Affairs and as dean of the faculty at Midwestern Seminary in Kansas City, was elected as the new executive director-treasurer on a secret ballot by a vote of 16-13. The voting was preceded by intensive questioning on such issues as abortion, capital punishment, and women in ministry.

Baker's answers were not satisfactory to the extreme pro-life advocates among the trustees. Baker took a middle of the road stand: somewhat pro-choice, but chiefly pro-life. He was firmly opposed to abortion on demand as a means of birth control, but felt that abortion was permissible in cases of (1) rape, (2) incest, (3) a threat to the mother's health or life, and (4) perhaps in the case of a severely damaged, incapacitated fetus.[185]

At the time of Baker's election, the pro-life members of the Commission's board of trustees were displeased, and said Baker would only be able to serve for six months. Additional members of the takeover faction were due on the trustee board by the next meeting. Baker, although aware of the situation, chose to go ahead with flawed approval, and began his term. He made valiant efforts to enhance the image of the Commission by giving attention to abortion and related issues, including a two-day conference.

At the end of six months, in September of 1987, Baker was given a dubious 15-15 vote of confidence, and remained in office.[186] In mid-1988, however, Baker resigned to accept the call as pastor of the First Baptist Church, Pineville, Louisiana. CLC associate director Robert Parham, now director of the Baptist Center for Ethics, was named interim executive director.

A search committee, now controlled by fundamentalists, nominated Richard Land, vice-president for academic affairs at Criswell College, to be the new executive-director. Land was a strong anti-abortionist, opposed to women's ordination, a proponent of capital punishment, rejected pacifism, and was an inerrantist. He was elected by a vote of 23-2, reflecting the changes in the board of trustees, and took office in October 1988.

As a reflection of this change, some trustees exhibited a lack of previous denominational involvement and a curious understanding of Christian ethics. One trustee failed to recognize the names of long-time denominational leaders, in particular, the president of the national Woman's Missionary Union. Curtis W. Caine, a new CLC trustee from Jackson, Mississippi, told the press at the September 1988 CLC trustee meeting, that "integration shouldn't have happened," "Martin Luther King was a fraud," and apartheid in South Africa "doesn't exist anymore and was beneficial when it did." His opinions were immediately rejected by the Texas Baptist Christian Life Commission[187] and repudiated in a resolution adopted at the Mississippi Baptist Convention in November 1988.[188]

Several months later, with Caine pointedly abstaining, the CLC adopted a six-point resolution calling for opposition to racism "whenever and wherever it occurs." The resolution had been proposed earlier by Richard Land at a race-relations conference sponsored by the CLC January 16, 1989 on the occasion of Martin Luther Kings' birthday.[189]

CLC associate director Robert C. Parham resigned from the commission in 1991 and formed the Baptist Center for Ethics to respond to ethical concerns of moderate Southern Baptists.[190]

In recent years, CLC Director Land and other new SBC leaders have become more vocal in political affairs. Instead of speaking merely to moral issues, they have intentionally courted right-wing politicians in an effort to further their agenda.

In 1986, a National Affairs Briefing, hosted by fundamentalist Baptist layman Ed McAteer, was held at the Pyramid Hotel in Memphis, Tenn. Six Republican candidates and one Libertarian candidate accepted invitations to attend. Along with Land and Adrian Rogers, pastor of the Bellevue Baptist Church in suburban Memphis (and McAteer's pastor), Beverly LaHaye, president of Concerned Women for America and Ralph Reed of the Christian Coalition, were among those participating in the meeting.[191]

The Florida Baptist Convention appointed a Baptist as state legislative consultant in 1996. His task is to monitor legislation and inform Florida Baptists regarding issues of moral concern. Many moderates believe he also serves as a lobbyist to represent the political opinions of State Convention leadership.

Fundamentalist leaders within and outside the Convention have supported the Republican Party, on the assumption that the Republicans were more supportive of their conservative social agenda. The Southern Baptist Conventions have in fact been jokingly referred to as "the Republican Party at prayer." Many Republican politicians, however, have been reluctant to fully embrace the religious right, for fear of alienating the larger "centrist" vote. Conservative religious leaders grow increasingly frustrated with their repeated experience of being "courted" and then "dumped" at the alter. James Dobson, president of Focus on the Family and a speaker at the 1998 SBC is quoted in *The Washington Post* as saying, "If the [Republican] party doesn't respond, `there's going to be trouble down the road. A lot of our constituents will stay home in '98; some will vote for another party'."[192]

21. The Sunday School Board/ LifeWay Christian Resources

Lloyd Elder, who became president of the Baptist Sunday School Board (BSSB) in 1984, succeeded Grady Cothen. Prior to becoming president elect of the BSSB in 1983, he was executive vice president at Southwestern Baptist Theological Seminary in Fort Worth. As BSSB president, Elder was regularly criticized by fundamentalist trustees who charged him with being involved on the moderate side in the Convention controversy.

James Larry Holly, a Beaumont, Texas physician and BSSB trustee, mailed more than forty pages of criticisms and questions of Elder in July 1989, and called for Elder's censure. A motion by another trustee to fire Elder was withdrawn after a lengthy discussion in which Elder was rebuked for alleged involvement in denominational politics.[193]

The following year, trustees voted not to publish a history of the Sunday School Board by Southwestern Seminary church history professor Leon McBeth. McBeth said he understood that trustees were upset the book did not deal harshly with Elder. Trustees shredded all copies, except one which was placed in the agency's archives.[194] In response, the Southwestern Seminary faculty unanimously affirmed McBeth and his scholarship.[195]

Holly, the disgruntled trustee from Beaumont, mailed a 233-page report, in December 1990, to the trustees' general administrative committee criticizing Elder's handling of the McBeth manuscript, which Holly said, made it look "like a lot of red-neck, right-wing, reactionary, fundamentalist trustees withdrew a book they did not like."[196]

In a called meeting of the BSSB trustees, Elder announced he would retire early effective January 31, 1992, or 30 days after his successor was elected. An amendment to the agreement so that Elder would retire "immediately" was defeated. Elder, 58, was named to the H. Franklin Paschall Chair of Biblical Studies and Preaching at Belmont College in Nashville in June 1991.[197]

Fundamentalist Texas pastor and 1983-84 SBC president Jimmy Draper succeeded Elder as BSSB president after his election in July 1991. Like other fundamentalist leaders elected as agency heads, Draper said new BSSB staff would be required to affirm inerrancy.[198] Draper immediately began reorganizing the BSSB to reshape it into a publishing house with a fundamentalist message. He also began to trim staff to make the Board more financially solid. A number of senior staff resigned or took early retirement (voluntarily and involuntarily). A total of 159 employees agreed to early retirement in November 1992 alone.[199]

Messengers to the 1998 SBC approved a name change for the Sunday School Board to LifeWay Christian Resources of the Southern Baptist Convention.

22. The Baptist Press

The right of every Baptist to know is based on the equality of believers in Christ Jesus and upon the democratic nature of our church and denominational life. Every believer has a right to serve his or her God, his or her church, and his or her denomination intelligently. This can be done only as the right to know is respected. — W. G. Stracener, editor of the Florida Baptist Witness from 1959-70 in 1957 speech to Orange Blossom Baptist Association.[200]

Baptist Press, the news service of the Southern Baptist Convention, provides daily releases, news features and photographs to 37 Baptist papers, to other religious journals, and to the secular press. The press service is an arm of the SBC Executive Committee.

A long-term participant in and observer of Baptist life has wisely stated, "The largest, most productive and most cost-efficient communications effort of each and all the Baptist state conventions is the 37 state Baptist newspapers."[201]

Almost without exception, Baptist Press consistently received the highest commendation from its many and varied constituencies. These included college and university journalism professors, religion writers and reporters from the secular media, public relations professionals, and denominational leaders.

Executive Committee trustee Paul Pressler was a notable exception to this generally positive evaluation. This powerful leader of the takeover effort had been an intense critic of Baptist Press for many years. He was not pleased with former Baptist Press director W. C. Fields; nor was he pleased with Alvin C. "Al" Shackleford, the committed, capable, and experienced director of Baptist Press who took office in March 1987.

Periodically, Pressler expressed his negative evaluation of Baptist Press's work by letter to the staff or to other persons who might have influence with the staff. Often, he insisted that "public apology" be made to him for Baptist Press statements concerning himself or the takeover effort he was leading.

In an encounter with Shackleford during the May 1987 Conference on Biblical Inerrancy at Ridgecrest, North Carolina, Pressler angrily waved a Baptist Press news release in Shackleford's face that reported, in a thoroughly fair and professional way, what had been said at one of the sessions. As the two men stood in the Ridgecrest cafeteria line, Pressler demanded, "What are you going to do about this? I want to know what you're going to do about this."

In its February 1988 session, the SBC Executive Committee received the report and recommendations of a special committee that had been authorized at the 1987 SBC in St. Louis to evaluate Baptist Press. The Executive Committee took action "generally affirming" Baptist Press. Also during the February meeting, the Southern Baptist Press Association, composed primarily of Baptist state paper editors, commended Baptist Press for "a fair, accurate, and comprehensive job of reporting events in Southern Baptist life."

Despite these affirmations, Pressler continued his determined effort to restrict the freedom of Baptist Press during a meeting of the Executive Committee during the June 1988 SBC. He chose that time because he knew that trustees elected during the SBC would be fundamentalists and would probably support his effort. However, his motion to add restrictive guidelines to govern Baptist Press failed — but only by a vote of 31-29.

Following those events at the 1988 SBC in San Antonio, Ed Briggs, president of the Religious Newswriters Association and religion editor of the *Richmond Times-Dispatch*, sent a strong letter to the chairman of the SBC Executive Committee. The members of the Religious Newswriters Association cover religion for newspapers, news magazines, and wire services in the United States and Canada.

In his letter, subsequently published,[202] Briggs expressed the praise of American newswriters in lavish terms: "Baptist Press enjoys high credibility, if not the highest, when compared to news operations of other American denominations."

Briggs also expressed the newswriters' uneasiness about the restrictive guidelines Pressler proposed in San Antonio. "We are concerned any time efforts are made to stifle freedom of expression and place restrictions and limitations on news organizations." The letter went on to invoke the example of "Baptist saints who faced jail rather than bow down to dictated religion."

An emasculated Baptist Press of managed and manipulated news would be an affront to all persons who believe in the competence of the individual to deal directly with God, the priesthood of every believer, religious liberty, and local church autonomy. An emasculated Baptist Press would also mean that Southern Baptists would be far less likely to learn anything about their denomination's affairs — except the things the controlling group wanted them to know.

Pressler and other fundamentalists continued to claim Baptist Press wrote stories which "persecuted" fundamentalists.[203] Baptist Press reporters are hired by and can be fired by the persons and agencies about which they write. Pressure is, therefore, on reporters to write stories with a certain "spin" to reflect well on supervisors and their agencies. Only the most courageous reporters write the truth, good or bad, and they quickly become targets.

Finally, in June 1990, the administrative committee of the SBC Executive Committee directed Executive Committee President Harold Bennett to ask for the resignations of Al Shackleford, 58, and Dan Martin, 52. They refused to resign and wrote a Baptist Press story on the request.

In response, the outraged officers of the SBC Executive Committee demanded a called meeting on July 17, 1990. The meeting cost a reported $45,500, including $500 for five armed guards from the Nashville Metro Police Department, who guarded the doors to the meeting room. The two embattled men were again asked to resign, and again they refused. As 200 concerned editors, agency personnel, pastors, lay persons, and others sang hymns outside the closed doors of the conference room, Shackleford and Martin were fired "effective immediately."[204]

Of the firing, Don McGregor, editor of the Mississippi *Baptist Record*, wrote, "Today, we have seen the final destruction of freedom of the press among Southern Baptists... They were fired because the majority of SBC executive committee does not want a free-flowing, objective and accurate news service."[205]

Immediately after the firing was announced, a Nashville attorney, who said he was speaking on behalf of "concerned editors, pastors and laypersons," announced the formation of a new press service, to be called the Associated Baptist Press (ABP).

Dan Martin was named interim director with a launch date of September 1990. Don McGregor, who had retired as editor of the *Baptist Record*, was named executive director of ABP in March 1991.[206] Greg Warner, associate editor of *The Florida Baptist Witness*, was named editor of ABP effective May 1, 1991.[207] After several years as a free-lance writer and pastor of a North Carolina church, Martin was named executive-director of Texans Who Care, a statewide anti-gambling coalition, in December 1992.[208]

Ed Young, SBC president, in an address to the SBC Executive Committee in early 1994, called for an end of "investigative reporting" by Christian editors and reporters, saying they should major on the "fabulous things" that are happening in the kingdom. Jack E. Brymer, Sr., editor of the *Florida Baptist Witness*, responded that "As long as Baptist leaders continue the use of "executive sessions" to cover-up their actions, Baptist journalism will need more, not less investigative reporting."[209]

After Young's speech, the SBC Christian Life Commission (CLC) severely criticized the *Biblical Recorder*, the newsjournal of the Baptist State Convention of North Carolina, in a four-page letter mailed to 3,547 North Carolina pastors at a cost of about $1,300. Baptist Press reported the mailing was the first time a SBC agency had sent a letter to state pastors chiding a state agency.[210]

The SBC Executive Committee began publishing SBC LIFE in 1993 to replace the *Baptist Program*, published since 1925. Since it is published by the Executive Committee, SBC LIFE, an official SBC publication, is a full-color public relations news journal with articles to promote the fundamentalist agenda and attack all opposing views within the SBC. In the June-July 1994 issue, editor Mark Coppenger blasted the CBF, Religious News Service, Christianity Today, Baptist Press and Baptist state papers, with the exception of the *Indiana Baptist*, with what one Baptist state paper editor said was a "scissors and paste tirade."[211]

In December 1987, Jack U. Harwell, long-time editor of *The Christian Index*, state paper for Georgia, took early retirement in protest of a fundamentalist board of directors restricting editorial freedom. He was named editor of BAPTISTS TODAY in June 1988 and served in that position until his retirement at the end of 1997.

In September 1994, Jack Brymer, editor of Florida's state paper, *The Baptist Witness*, cited threats to his professional integrity before resigning in protest of continued attempts by the board of directors to restrict his editorial freedom. Among other things, the board was pressuring him not to use news stories from Associated Baptist Press.[212] Brymer was named to a newly created post of director of publications at Samford University in Alabama in September 1995.

23. Independent Baptist Papers

One of the marked features of the current Southern Baptist controversy has been the fact that it has helped give rise to several independent Baptist newspapers — "independent" in the sense that they are not controlled by one of the state Baptist conventions or by the SBC Executive Committee.

In 1973, in the aftermath of the *Broadman Commentary* controversy, the first of the independent Southern Baptist papers was begun. *The Southern Baptist Journal* was begun by the Baptist Faith and Message group in a meeting at First Baptist Church, Atlanta. William Powell was named editor. It is strident fundamentalism without any qualification.

In 1980, a new independent paper often regarded as the voice for the Pressler-Patterson group, *The Southern Baptist Advocate*, was begun in Dallas under the editorship of Paige Patterson's brother-in-law, Russell Kaemmerling. Kaemmerling resigned in 1986. Robert M. Tenery, pastor of the Burkemont Baptist Church in Morganton, North Carolina, was named editor. In the 90s Tennery also publishes *Baptists United News*, a fundamentalist newspaper focusing on North Carolina.[213]

Jerry Falwell, an independent Baptist and popular speaker at fundamentalist SBC meetings, published *The Fundamentalist Journal* from 1982 through 1989. The periodical regularly featured stories about Southern Baptist fundamentalists.[214]

Other Fundamentalist papers started during this era include the following:

- *The Southern Baptist Watchman* started in November 1991 by Walter Carpenter.

- *The Texas Baptist*, also edited by Walter Carpenter.

- *The Southern Baptist Communicator* started in 1991, edited by Fred Powell. Powell urged fundamentalists to defeat J. Truett Gannon, pastor of Smoke Rise Baptist Church in Stone Mountain, Georgia, as president of the Georgia Baptist Convention. Gannon was reelected by 68 votes.[215]

- *The Baptist Observer*, started in 1992 by Alabama Baptists, as part of a statewide effort to elect Fred Lackey president of the state convention. Lackey was seen as part of the effort to decide the future direction of Samford University.[216]

- *The Baptist Banner*, launched in 1994 in Virginia. Well-known fundamentalist T. C. Pinckney was editor.[217]

- *The SBC of Virginia Update* has been published by Southern Baptist Conservatives of Virginia, since the formed their own state convention in 1996.

With exceptions, these newspapers were generally short-lived or have been published irregularly.

In April 1983, a number of Southern Baptist moderates began a new publication, SBC TODAY. Walker L. Knight, a career journalist, director of editorial services at the Home Mission Board, and long-time editor of *Home Missions*, was named editor of the new paper. Knight's courageous stance for racial justice and reconciliation during the turbulent civil rights era of the 1950s and 1960s showed him to be a leader among Baptists. Knight did not conceive the publication as a mouthpiece for one side in a conflict. From the beginning, sometimes to the annoyance of financial backers, he edited the paper as "independent" in a second sense, namely, as a national newspaper in its own right for all Baptists. The editorial position, however, was to be unmistakably moderate.

SBC TODAY (its name was changed to BAPTISTS TODAY in August 1991 to reflect the wider scope of its news) is the only one of the independent papers to have maintained a regular schedule of publication. It also distinguishes its news content from its opinion pieces with a care and consistency that is not approached by the other independent papers.

In June 1988, Jack U. Harwell became editor of SBC TODAY. Harwell, before going to SBC TODAY, was editor of one of the largest-circulation state Baptist papers, *The Christian Index* of Georgia, for 21 years. Harwell retired from BAPTISTS TODAY in December 1997 at age 65.

In 1998, directors of BAPTISTS TODAY approved a contract with Smyth & Helyws in Macon, Ga. to manage the monthly newspaper from its offices. BAPTISTS TODAY moved its offices to Macon in September 1998.

Moderate Southern Baptists published other newspapers, including *The Call, Dallas*, '85, edited by Larry Dipboye in Louisville, Kentucky, to encourage attendance at the 1985 Dallas SBC. *The Baptist Laity Journal* was published from 1985 until 1990 in Texas. Texas Baptist Committed also publishes a newsletter.

24. Foreign Mission Board / International Mission Board

Career missionary R. Keith Parks was elected Foreign Mission Board president in 1980. He would serve the FMB a total of 38 years. During his 13 years as FMB president, the Board entered 40 new countries to give the FMB 3,918 missionaries in 126 countries.[218]

As early as 1985, Parks spoke out courageously to contend that the controversy in the denomination was damaging our mission efforts. He described our missionaries as hostages to the conflict. He urged that nothing be allowed to weaken or interfere with our mission work. He reiterated that the missionaries are fully committed, and that they believe the Bible, holding it to be the sufficient, certain and authoritative Word of God.

Despite these assurances, the takeover group continued to question the Biblical orthodoxy of some missionaries. Fundamentalists were also at a loss over what to do about Keith Parks. He was known as an outstanding preacher of unquestioned missionary zeal and yet he did not support their cause. Both Parks and his missionaries became the targets of fundamentalist concern.

Problems began to develop after trustees dropped a requirement that all missionaries have at least one year of study in a Southern Baptist seminary. The change opened the door for missionary candidates from independent fundamentalist institutions to be appointed. Some fundamentalist missionaries challenged the orthodoxy of their colleagues on the field. In the summer of 1988, Michael Willett, a missionary ending his language training for service in South America, was fired over what was described as a "doctrinal" issue.[219] Reports indicate that another missionary, a graduate of a non-SBC seminary, kept extensive notes on Willett's views and informed on him.[220]

In 1990, new FMB trustee chair Bill Hancock affirmed Parks, saying, Parks is "God's man for this hour," and "we as trustees unanimously and uncompromisingly affirm Keith Parks as our leader of the FMB."[221] In 1991, Parks stated his wish to continue serving as FMB president until 1995 to maintain momentum and lead preparations up to the launch date of his "Mission 21" vision, which would take the FMB into the 21st century, but the drive to fulfill a fundamentalist agenda forged onward.

At their October 1991 meeting, FMB trustees voted to defund the Baptist Theological Seminary in Ruschlikon, Switzerland. The seminary was founded by Southern Baptists in 1949. It had come under increasing criticism from fundamentalists for its alleged liberal faculty. European, as well as many SBC, Baptist leaders expressed shock at the unexpected loss of $365,000, 40 percent of the seminary's budget. Two professors at the Spanish Baptist Seminary in Madrid, Spain called the cutoff "a radical measure that has negative influence on cooperative ministries with Baptists in Europe." FMB trustee Paige Patterson said, "This board is not going to be impacted by the protests of a few Europeans."[222] The trustees refused to restore the deleted funds in a December 1991 meeting.

The Baptist Theological Seminary, now supported by the Cooperative Baptist Fellowship, several state conventions, and numerous individuals, announced in 1993 a name change to the International Baptist Theological Seminary and its move to Prague, the Czech Republic, in 1995. North Carolina Baptist Men announced they would serve as stateside coordinators for the building and renovation of the seminary's new facilities; Baptist groups in other states and countries have provided assistance for the project.[223]

In reaction to Keith Parks' expressed desire to remain at the FMB helm until 1995, a motion to form a search committee to seek Parks' successor was made and withdrawn at the October 1991 FMB trustee meeting. A reported motion to name a co-president with equal authority to Parks was defeated. Parks and FMB trustee chair Bill Hancock praised each other's leadership in a later press conference.[224]

But, after years of trying to please fundamentalist trustees, Parks announced in March 1992 his retirement effective in October 1992. The announcement came after 13 hours of intense, closed-door dialogue with FMB trustees.[225] Parks said he was not convinced trustees would give him the freedom to do his job. Some SBC fundamentalists have opposed Parks since he publicly opposed Charles Stanley's candidacy for SBC president in 1985. Parks had cited the minuscule giving to the SBC Cooperative Program by Stanley's First Baptist Church of Atlanta, as a sign that Stanley and his church did not wish to serve the Southern Baptist mission effort unless they could control it.[226]

A month after his resignation from the FMB, Parks joined the Cooperative Baptist Fellowship as missions coordinator. Bill Pinson, executive director of the Baptist General Convention of Texas, said of Parks, "At a time when numerous denominations were pulling back from foreign-missions efforts, Keith Parks was urging Southern Baptists to move forward. He helped Southern Baptists realize the extent of the world's lostness."[227] That worldwide vision was now being put to work on behalf of a more moderate community of Southern Baptists who were seeking a missions program they could support in good conscience.

In early 1993, Tom Elliff, Bailey Smith's brother-in-law and pastor of the First Southern Baptist Church of Del City, Oklahoma, declined the offer to become president of the FMB.[228] Elliff was elected SBC president in 1996 and 1997. FMB trustees elected career missionary Jerry Rankin, 41, as president in May 1993. Rankin was described as "sympathetic to the cause of SBC fundamentalists and committed to biblical inerrancy." FMB trustee Paul Pressler led an effort to derail Rankin's election, but Rankin was elected by a vote of 59-14.[229]

25. The Moderate Response to Fundamentalist Politics

The devastation left in the wake of the fundamentalist takeover is obvious to those Baptists who appreciate the freedom, diversity and openness of former days. There was a time when all Southern Baptists stood together in doing the work of the gospel. While we might have differed on how best to do this, we did not try to exclude each other from the opportunity to do ministry. The damage done to the cause of Christ by the fundamentalist takeover is incalculable. But the perceptive reader may be wondering where the moderates were as the fundamentalist juggernaut plowed forward. Was there any significant attempt to thwart the takeover before it went too far? What was the political response to this very political takeover?

An intentional effort to defeat the fundamentalist revolution eventually evolved, but moderates were slow to take up partisan politics within the convention. At the beginning of the controversy most of the Seminary leadership and most of the SBC agency leadership was made up of people who would later identify themselves as "moderates." They saw the election of Adrian Rogers and the political machinations of Paige Patterson and Judge Pressler as distasteful but not alarming. In retrospect these leaders were clearly overconfident. They had been in the vanguard of SBC leadership for many years, and assumed that they had built up a reservoir of trust in the denomination that could not be easily shaken. They assumed this new controversy was just another fundamentalist "tempest in a teapot", that would soon blow over. In any event, people of their view held most of the reins of power in the denomination. They felt they could "handle" the upstarts.

After the election of Bailey Smith to be SBC President at the 1980 convention with 51% of the vote on the first ballot, against 5 other non-aligned candidates, the moderates were shaken. Paul Pressler's announcement in September that a fundamentalist political strategy did indeed exist and that they were attempting to "go for the jugular" of the convention, galvanized moderates into action. Duke McCall, former President of Southern Seminary, encouraged Cecil Sherman, then Pastor of the First Baptist Church of Asheville, North Carolina, to launch a resistance movement. Dr. Sherman asked seventeen trusted leaders from various states to meet with him in Gatlinburg, Tennessee in late September of 1980. The group that met there became known, somewhat humorously, as the "Gatlinburg Gang."

Together, these men developed their own strategy for a "get out the vote" campaign. Their goal was to defeat the Pressler-Patterson machine by electing a consensus candidate that would be acceptable to a broad spectrum of Southern Baptists. Many of the candidates put forward by the moderates over the next few years were quite theologically conservative, but were not willing to shut all moderates out of the denomination. The "get out the vote" strategy was simple enough, and while it grew in size over the next few years, it never became much more complex. They sought out viable candidates and generally agreed to support one in particular before each upcoming national convention. They elected a national coordinator for their movement. They also selected state coordinators who would, in turn, recruit coordinators in the local Baptist Associations. Based on the number of messengers who promised to go and vote for a moderate candidate, they estimated their chances and focused additional efforts to recruit more messengers from weaker areas.

Their rhetorical strategy was simple as well. Moderates described themselves as denominational loyalists and friends of missions. They also presented themselves as the "true conservatives" because they wanted to maintain the Southern Baptist traditions of soul freedom and the Priesthood of all believers. In contrast fundamentalists were shown to be violating traditional Baptist freedoms. Moderates accused the fundamentalists of diverting money, time and energy from "Bold Mission Thrust" program, an attempt to reach everyone with a gospel witness before the end of the century. Moderates pointed out that the charges of rampant liberalism in the denomination were vastly exaggerated. In tandem with this, they declared that the fundamentalist movement was primarily a grab for power, with theological issues being used as a smokescreen. Moderates showcased the ethical transgressions in the political activity of the fundamentalists.

They also pointed out that the whole political enterprise launched by the fundamentalists was an exercise in worldly politics, far removed from the kindness and civility of previous years. Even the stern fundamentalist patriarch at the First Baptist Church of Dallas, W.A. Criswell, was disturbed by the tactics of the takeover faction. He declared in 1980 that the methods used by his associate, Paige Patterson were "those of a different world."[230]

The efforts and arguments of the moderates persuaded thousands of dedicated Baptists to rally against the takeover effort, and the substantial moderate vote from 1981 through 1990 shows quite clearly that fundamentalists were not telling the truth when they insisted that a vast majority of Southern Baptists welcomed their efforts to make the convention over. However, while the moderate effort was valiant and strong it was never enough to derail the takeover. The fundamentalists had to fight hard for it, but they won every election for president from 1979 onward. In some cases the vote was very close, and on several occasions the convention registered more messengers than had ever registered in Southern Baptist history. Noting that there was no "moderate candidate" offered in 1979 or 1980, the vote percentage for the fundamentalist candidate each year of a non-incumbent election is shown below. Incumbent years are not listed because it is a Southern Baptist tradition to re-elect incumbent presidents to a second year term, unless there has been some scandal or malfeasance in office.

1979	Adrian Rogers	51.36%
1980	Bailey Smith	51.67%
1982	Jimmy Draper	56.97%
1984	Charles Stanley	52.18%
1986	Adrian Rogers	54.22%
1988	Jerry Vines	50.53%
1990	Morris Chapman	57.68%

Each year from 1981 through 1990 (with the exception of 1983), the moderate group that grew out of the Gatlinburg meeting supported a particular candidate. This, of course, did not stop others from running, so in some years there were other candidates splitting the non-fundamentalist vote. The candidates offered by the moderate movement were:

1981 Abner McCall
           defeated in Los Angeles, with 39.30%
1982 Duke McCall
           defeated in New Orleans, with 43.03%
1983 No candidate
1984 Grady Cothen
           defeated in Kansas City with 26.28%
1985 Winfred Moore
           defeated in Dallas, with 44.7%
1986 Winfred Moore
           defeated in Atlanta with 45.78%
1987 Richard Jackson
           defeated in St. Louis with 40.03%
1988 Richard Jackson
           defeated in San Antonio with 48.32%
1989 Dan Vestal
           defeated in Las Vegas with 43.39%
1990 Dan Vestal
           defeated in New Orleans, with 42.32%

As one can see, with the exception of 1981 and 1984 when the moderate vote was deeply split, moderates never polled less than 40% of the national vote, even when running against incumbents who could rely on Southern Baptist tradition to be re-elected. James Slatton, one of the key leaders of the moderate political efforts observes that "The really remarkable thing about the moderate movement was not that it failed throughout ten years to defeat fundamentalist presidential candidates, but that so many people were mobilized by so few with so limited resources. In the words of the late Donald Harbuck at the Los Angeles SBC, 'I've never lost in such great numbers before.'"[231]

The moderates lost "the struggle for the soul of the SBC" as Walter Shurden puts it, for several reasons. To begin with, they had to play "catch-up" against an opposition that was already well organized and had won two major elections in 1979 and 1980. On the strength of those victories, the fundamentalists were well ahead of the moderates in understanding the mechanics of how to dominate the conventions. Their troops came early, got the best blocks of hotel rooms near the convention centers, and sat in the seats closest to the rostrum for best effect in both voice and hand votes.

Incumbency also has its advantages in planning and administrating the conventions. As you will note from the list above, the vast majority of the conventions in those key years were held west of the Mississippi River. All of them, with the exception of the convention in Atlanta, were held far away from the moderate's strongest numerical base, along the eastern seaboard. Distance is always a factor in getting people to attend national conventions. The locations of conventions were often planned some years in advance, so it is hard to know how much of this was intentionally planned for political effect. One thing is certain, there are far more fundamentalist Baptists in the American west and deep south, where the vast majority of these conventions were held. This worked strongly to the advantage of the take-over faction.

Another advantage of incumbency is the extensive power of the convention president as chair of the meeting. Each of the editors of this booklet has witnessed high-handed and partisan use of the chair in everything from the recognition of speakers to parliamentary procedure rulings. The rulings of the president could be challenged and appealed to a parliamentarian, kept near the platform for just such disputes. However, even the selection of the parliamentarian is in the control of those who run the convention. That advantage is seen quite clearly in a celebration following the 1990 Convention in New Orleans. Following their massive and rather final defeat of the moderates, Paige Patterson and others went to the Café Du Monde in the French Quarter to celebrate their victory. Patterson and Pressler were given framed certificates honoring their achievements. The convention parliamentarian, supposedly neutral and from another denomination, was present for the celebration, and even called it to order! When his presence at this meeting was challenged as inappropriate, he first explained that he was "just passing by, picking up an order of doughnuts." When the challengers pointed out that the parliamentarian had actually been seen arriving at Café Du Monde in a limousine with the convention president, he amended his story to say that he was on "twenty-four hour call" and therefore obliged to accompany the president wherever he went. When one messenger tried to tell the story of what he had seen at Café Du Monde to the convention the following day, he was deterred. Twice the president refused to recognize him and twice his microphone was turned off.[232] Such abuse of the chair was common all during the takeover.

Another reason for the failure of the moderate political response is that very early on the fundamentalists had convinced many Baptists that they held the moral high ground. As James Slatton observes, "they had 'prayer meetings' not political rallies, and they were 'led of the Spirit' to nominate 'godly' men for office."[233] Thus, they often obscured the worldly political nature of their activities. Their rhetoric, accusing denominational leaders and seminary professors of "liberalism," and their passionate call to "save the Bible" within the convention, was exactly the kind of white-hot language that sweeps a crowd off their feet into a glorious sense of mission. It was much like the inflammatory rhetoric of Eugene McCarthy's hunt for communists, and politicians of another era who used the language of racial prejudice to get in power. Fundamentalist language engaged the heart, while deceptively disengaging the mind.

The moderate position was a harder sell precisely because it was "moderate." Fundamentalist language was not. Educated fundamentalists might qualify their statements about the Bible more carefully in a classroom setting, but on the political stump, when they fiercely declared the Bible "inerrant" they stirred the passions of many Bible-believing Baptists. The moderate position, more thoughtful and more truthful, was better crafted for the classroom. Few ever learned how to present moderate beliefs in the language of a rally. So, as the fundamentalists proclaimed the Bible inerrant, moderates were either silent or too cerebral, and gave the impression that these accusations of heresy were true. To say, "well, let's think about this more carefully," is hardly going to bring your basic Baptist to his feet in passionate commitment. Unwilling to cast the basic subjects of the controversy in moral and political language, moderates were left with trying to discredit the ethics and the distinctive Baptist-ness of their opponents. They presented the controversy as merely a power struggle. True believers in the fundamentalist camp were generally unfazed by this approach and many non-fundamentalists saw such attacks as "mean-spirited."

This, of course, brings us to another problem for the moderate political response. Moderates found the whole political nature of the controversy mean-spirited and distasteful in the extreme. They saw any response in kind as sinking to the level of the enemy. They regarded such partisan and exclusionary politics as beneath the dignity of civil Christian churchmanship; beyond the pale of both Baptist freedom and Christian love — their most cherished Biblical values. While the typical fundamentalist layperson was caught up in the excitement of a "revolution for God," moderates wrestled with how far to go in fighting back. Hence, many moderates were loathe to rise to the occasion. In practical terms, this meant they never raised quite enough money or quite enough votes to rival their opponents in the contest.

Far from being motivated by white-hot political rhetoric, the Gatlinburg Gang and other moderate leaders were often intentionally discouraged from political organizing by their own allies. Cecil Sherman tells of how one moderate leader warned him in 1981 that moderate political organizing would only make things worse, and that they should simply wait for "the pendulum to swing back." A major denominational executive told him, "Stop what you are doing Cecil, we can handle these people." When the Seminary presidents offered "the Glorieta Statement" in 1986, affirming Biblical inerrancy, in the hope that their schools would not be further attacked, Dr. Sherman protested to one of the Seminary presidents who was later summarily fired by fundamentalist trustees. That president told him, "Cecil, you are more trouble to us than they are."[234] Such responses on the part of people they were trying to help did not exactly create a "Go get 'em, you can do it!" spirit.

Some prominent and influential pastors failed to speak out when it might have done more good because they were reluctant to join the rough-and-tumble of a political fight. Other moderates were afraid of being painted as liberals by the other side, and thus losing their jobs. The moderate political movement that did evolve from the Gatlinburg meeting was loose knit, with occasionally changing leadership. The fundamentalists were tightly organized with an almost military discipline, and had focused, consistent leadership with a clear vision and a clear strategy that they stayed with throughout their campaign. Cecil Sherman points out that if the moderate leaders had been more authoritarian in their approach, no one would have followed them, since moderates by nature resist the kind of authoritarian, lock-step approach common to fundamentalists. For all these reasons, the energy and momentum were never sufficient in the moderate movement to defeat a dedicated opposition willing to make great sacrifices.

There were, however, many great men and women of the moderate Baptist community who fought the good fight to the bitter end for freedom and truth. Great sacrifices in time, money, and career advancement were made by those faithful Christians. Here follows a year by year look at the efforts they made and the difficulties they faced from the 1981 Convention to the 1990 defeat in New Orleans.

1981

Fundamentalist candidate Bailey Smith makes conciliatory statements in the spring before the convention, thus taking momentum away from the moderate response. He is re-elected over Abner McCall, then President of Baylor University. ·

1982

The moderate effort is blunted by failure to unify the non-fundamentalist vote. The fundamentalist candidate, Jimmy Draper, was elected over the formal moderate candidate, Duke McCall, past President of Southern Seminary, and two popular Louisiana pastors: John Sullivan and Perry Sanders. SBC agency heads, previously staying at arms length from the moderate movement, become convinced of the need for moderate political action.

1983

The convention is held in Pittsburgh. Facing a popular incumbent in a remote location, the moderate political network decides not to field a candidate. A new pre-convention fellowship, "Friends of Missions," is held as an alternative to the fundamentalist-dominated Pastor's Conference.

1984

The moderate network has lost momentum, partly due to the failure to field a candidate the previous year in Pittsburg, and partly because Foy Valentine, then Director of the Christian Life Commission, has declared that he will coordinate the election of his own candidate, Grady Cothen, then President of the Southern Baptist Sunday School Board. John Sullivan, of Shreveport, Louisiana also runs. Valentine employs a professional political consultant to organize moderate messenger support. In Kansas City, fundamentalist candidate Charles Stanley is elected on the first ballot. Finally some of the seminary presidents are motivated to seek the help of the moderate network.

1985

Charles Stanley runs as an incumbent against Winfred Moore, with the moderate network back on line. But the appointment of a "Peace Committee" at the Dallas Convention again takes some of the momentum out of the moderate effort, as people hope a true peace can be negotiated. Everyone on the Peace Committee is prohibited from actively doing convention politics so this takes Cecil Sherman, appointed to that committee, out of circulation as the leader of the moderate movement. It is at this convention that James Slatton offers his resolution to restructure the Committee on Committees to be made up of State Convention Presidents and State WMU Directors. The motion is ruled out of order by Charles Stanley.

1986

Repeated meetings with the Peace Committee produce no results, so neither side stands down. In a desperate effort to save
their seminaries from fundamentalist domination, the seminary
presidents issue the Glorieta Statement, affirming Biblical inerrancy. This capitulation is deeply discouraging to the moderate
network, suggesting that the seminary presidents do not have
the will to stand with them in the conflict. Cecil Sherman resigns
from the Peace Committee in protest. A professional political
consultant is employed to advise and assist the moderate network. The Convention meets in Atlanta and affirms the Peace
Committee report, which will now become a fundamentalist
creedal measuring-stick for the hiring of convention personnel.
Moderate candidate Winfred Moore is again defeated, by the
original fundamentalist standard bearer, Adrian Rogers. At a
meeting of the moderate network at Mercer University in Macon, Georgia, some leaders determine that the effort to defeat a
seemingly ruthless and relentless fundamentalism is fruitless. The
Southern Baptist Alliance, later to become the Alliance of Baptists, grows from this conviction on the part of some that its
time to start creating something new rather than defending the
old SBC.

1987

The moderate political network begins to take on a more institu-
tional form in the organization of Baptists Committed to the
Southern Baptist Convention. (This organization, which still functions under the name "Baptists Committed" in some states, will
later become the foundation for the Cooperative Baptist Fellowship.) The moderates are, on the whole, discouraged by the
Glorieta Statement, the founding of the Alliance and the naive
belief among many that the "Peace Committee" report has settled
all the issues of the controversy. Fundamentalists have successfully suggested that anyone challenging their leadership after the
Peace Committee's work is anti-peace. The fact that the fundamentalists only want peace on their own terms is demonstrated
when the moderates offer a peace settlement. If the fundamen-

talists are satisfied with the Peace Committee's work, will they accept the idea of appointing the State Convention Presidents and State WMU leaders to the Committee on Committees? The fundamentalist's public refusal of this offer shows clearly that they are still pursuing the agenda of a full takeover of the denomination. The convention meets in St. Louis, where Adrian Rogers is re-elected to a 3rd term as president.

1988

Jerry Vines, co-Pastor of the First Baptist Church of Jacksonville, Florida, defeats Richard Jackson, 51% to 48%, the closest vote in the history of the controversy.

1989

The Convention meets in Las Vegas. Incumbent Jerry Vines defeats Daniel Vestal, a conservative leader who defends the moderate commitment to the Bible very well, and proves to be, despite his loss, one of the moderate's best campaigners.

1990

The moderates are handed their most devastating defeat of the controversy, as Dan Vestal is defeated in New Orleans by Morris Chapman by a wide margin of 57% to 43%. The defeat is doubly painful because this marks the eleventh election since the beginning of the controversy. Judge Pressler had determined early on that the fundamentalists would only have to win ten elections in a row to create a fundamentalist majority on every board and agency of the convention. This eleventh election seals the fundamentalist victory, and they celebrate at Café Du Monde in the French Quarter, where Judge Pressler and Paige Patterson had first conceived the whole plan for the takeover, many years prior. The moderates who have not invested all their hopes and energies in the Alliance of Baptists are feeling defeated and disenfranchised. The moderate network will not offer any further candidates for president of the Southern Baptist Convention. The war is over and most moderates completely abandon national SBC politics. Many no longer even go to the national conventions. Daniel Vestal calls for a meeting of moderates to be held in Atlanta in August, in order to determine a future direction for their vision of Baptist life. The unexpected 3,000 that show up become the foundation for the Cooperative Baptist Fellowship.

The new fellowships and organizations that began to formulate from 1986 forward have become a fresh hope for Baptists who value freedom and love over legalism and ultra-orthodoxy. The Alliance, the CBF and other groups have become places where the moderate vision of Baptist Christianity can be fleshed out. The following sections of this booklet tell the story of these new Baptist communities in greater detail, and the final developments beyond the 1990 Convention are described.

26. The Alliance of Baptists

By the mid 1980s it was already clear to many non-fundamentalists that the nature of the SBC had been changed by the success of the fundamentalist movement, and that things would not revert back to the "good old days" any time soon. Non-fundamentalists felt a hunger for fellowship with other Baptists of like heart and mind. They also sought a place to voice their concerns and an outlet for doing missions in a manner that would not violate their conscience. Finally, many were just tired of being labeled "the enemy" at Southern Baptist Convention meetings.

It should come as no surprise that the most progressive elements of the SBC, primarily located in Virginia and North Carolina, were the first to seek shelter from the fundamentalist storm, by creating the Southern Baptist Alliance in 1986. In 1990 some of the more centrist and conservative Southern Baptists formed a more traditional non-fundamentalist movement, the Cooperative Baptist Fellowship. A small number of the more traditionalist members of the Alliance have gravitated to the CBF, but for the most part, these two organizations have served different constituencies. Many of the people who formed the Alliance were never entirely comfortable with the SBC and rejoiced in the creation of a fresh Baptist voice. Many of the people in the CBF treasure their memories of the old SBC before the fundamentalist takeover. It is understandable that the traditionalists would have a numerically larger constituency.

The Alliance is content to serve a smaller community of believers, committed to serving as a sanctuary for non-traditional Baptists who want to do theology and ministry in the most radically non-traditional ways. The history of the Alliance has largely been one of giving more than taking. Their commitment to remain a "still, small voice" of conscience in Baptist life has given them freedom to take more risks and in the process they have unselfishly given many gracious gifts to the Baptist community.

The Alliance had its beginnings in November 1986, when Southern Baptists from fifteen states met at the Providence Baptist Church in Charlotte, North Carolina to form the Southern Baptist Alliance (SBA), "dedicated to the preservation of historic Baptist principles, freedoms and traditions and the continuance of ministry and mission within the Southern Baptist Convention."[235] The SBA changed its name to Alliance of Baptists, Inc. in March 1992.[236]

In its seven-point covenant, the Alliance committed itself to the freedom of the individual to read and interpret the Bible; to the freedom of the local church to shape its own life and mission (for example, in ordaining women and men for ministry); and to cooperation with believers everywhere in expressing the Gospel.

In addition, the seven-point covenant includes a commitment to the servant role of leadership within the congregation; to theological education characterized by reverence for biblical authority and respect for open inquiry and responsible scholarship; and to proclamation of the Gospel that calls people to repentance, faith, and social justice. The final commitment is to a free church in a free state, neither using the other for its purposes.[237]

Stan Hastey, the son of SBC home missionaries, was elected as the Alliance's first full-time executive director in January 1989.

At the same time, offices were moved from Charlotte to Washington, D. C. Hastey, a journalist and administrator of considerable stature, had served fifteen years with the Baptist Joint Committee for Public Affairs. He had also been bureau chief for Baptist Press in Washington, D. C. Jeannette Holt has served as the very able assistant director for many years.

By February 1989, the Alliance had 44,000 members. Three thousand were individual members from 41 states, and the remainder were in 73 member churches in 13 states. In addition to these churches that had voted to join, other churches aligned themselves by contributing to the Alliance. The Alliance had, by this time, published its first book, *Being Baptist Means Freedom*, which was edited by Alan Neely.

The Alliance also committed itself in March 1989, if sufficient funds could be raised, to establish a theological seminary in Richmond, Virginia. Many Southern Baptists felt a need for a new seminary in the south, connected to their heritage, that could be more theologically trustworthy than the seminaries taken over by the fundamentalist movement. It was proposed that the new institution would enroll a maximum of 50 students per year, or 150 altogether. The seminary would be in consortium with one American Baptist and two Presbyterian theological schools in the city.[238]

The dream of a seminary in Richmond was realized when, in September 1991, the Baptist Theological Seminary at Richmond opened with Thomas H. Graves as president.[239] The seminary graduated its first students, all transfers from SBC seminaries, in May 1993. The Baptist Theological Seminary at Richmond is the only moderate Baptist seminary serving Southern Baptists that is not connected with a Baptist university, (with the exception of Central Seminary in Kansas City, which had been in existence as an American Baptist Seminary for many years.)

In its early years, the Alliance existed primarily for fellowship and a safe place to express the concerns of progressive Baptists. As various "orphaned" ministries were abandoned by the SBC they came to the Alliance for help. The first Alliance missions budget was passed in 1988, and implemented in 1989. The first mission funds were primarily designed to assist the Baptist Joint Committee and to provide pastoral assistance for mission churches ineligible to receive assistance from the SBC, because the pastor was either a woman or a divorced person. The Alliance's 1994 annual budget was $246,173; its 1998 budget was approximately $300,000.

The Cooperative Baptist Fellowship was born in 1991, and in 1992 there were serious talks of a merger between the two organizations. The merger did not take place. As the two bodies studied the possibility they realized that they really served slightly different communities of Baptists. Leaders realized they would both feel freer to be themselves without a merger.

In light of that, the Alliance offered all of its missionary concerns to the CBF, so there would be no confusion about the locus of moderate Baptist missions. The CBF accepted some of these mission enterprises but not all of them. The alliance decided they could not abandon their orphaned ministries, and determined to continue with a modest missions program, geared to helping the most needy and worthwhile missionary dreams in their community of concern. The Alliance missions program is extremely small by comparison with the SBC and CBF, but they give hope for the survival of Baptist mission programs that could not find a home anywhere else. The Alliance provides grants to various worthwhile causes, with no strings attached. They treat their mission friends with dignity and trust their leadership to spend the grants with wisdom.[240]

Stan Hastey sees the Alliance's role as "admittedly the most progressive of Baptists — people not afraid to take unpopular stands."[241] Hastey frequently describes the Alliance as a "think-tank" for new ideas in Baptist life, and a "seedbed" for the nurture of new ministries that are often taken over later by those who can better afford to fund them as they grow. The Alliance has been very intentional about allying itself with the oppressed, the disenfranchised, the poor and the powerless. Typically their first question in doing missions has been, "Who are the weakest and most powerless among us? Who needs an advocate here for justice and hope?"

With that in mind they have allied themselves with such needs as the Fraternity of Baptist Churches of Cuba, the Baptist Convention of Zimbabwe, the Baptist Peace Fellowship and Baptist Women in Ministry. They have provided pastoral assistance to small Baptist Churches that do not qualify for Southern Baptist pastoral assistance. They have worked for racial reconciliation, justice for women in the workplace and the church and they have bravely stood up for decent and gracious treatment of even the most reviled and oppressed persons of our world. Particularly controversial has been their moral support for Alliance affiliated churches that have offered a more tolerant and compassionate approach to homosexual church members.

Wherever Southern Baptists have abandoned mission models that do not square with church-planting and direct evangelism, the Alliance has worked to rescue worthwhile expressions of Baptist love and Baptist intellect, supporting foreign seminaries, medical missions and inner city ministry centers. They have led Baptists to identify with the poor and needy by maintaining a passion for helping the weakest among us.

The Alliance is involved in continuing conversations with the United Church of Christ over common issues and has prepared an adult curriculum on justice issues, which became available in 1999. The Alliance's annual Convocation has been held in March in different areas of the country. They have found that this date frequently conflicts with many state level meetings of the Cooperative Baptist Fellowship, so in the future the national convocations will be held on the first weekend after Easter. The 1999 convocation was held at Northminster Baptist Church in Richmond, Va., the meeting in the year 2000 was scheduled for University Baptist Church in Austin, Texas.

27. Cooperative Baptist Fellowship

If we stand for authentic Baptist beliefs in our local churches, in our state conventions, in our district associations, around the dinner table with friends and neighbors, we will find ourselves at odds with others at times. But, living as an authentic Baptist seems to inevitably bring conflict. — Gary Parker, Coordinator for Baptist Principles, CBF, Atlanta, Ga.[242]

After fundamentalists steamrolled moderates at the June 1990 SBC in New Orleans, Daniel Vestal, then pastor of the Dunwoody Baptist Church in Atlanta, called for a dialogue among moderate Baptists concerning their future in the SBC.[243] Over 3,000 Southern Baptists answered his call and met in Atlanta, Georgia August 23-25. Jimmy Allen, chair of Baptists Committed to the Southern Baptist Convention, a group organized in Texas in 1988, moderated at the Atlanta meeting. Those assembled created a new funding mechanism, the Baptist Cooperative Mission Program (BCMP). This funding mechanism was primarily used to channel mission giving specifically to those Southern Baptist causes that these moderate Baptists could support in good conscience. Dr. Vestal was named chair of the steering committee for "The Fellowship." They voted to meet again the following year.[244] Hettie Johnson, who had retired from the Home Mission Board, was named office manager for BCMP.

In May 1991, 6,000 Southern Baptists met again in Atlanta and adopted the name, Cooperative Baptist Fellowship (CBF), and approved a constitution, a budget, and a plan for world missions that went beyond the work of the Southern Baptist Convention. Vestal told the enthusiastic gathering, "We're here because we're sensing that God is doing a new thing."[245] The CBF for the present does not consider itself to be a separate convention and most participants don't see it as a separate denominational entity, but rather an alternative missionary society for those who prefer not to invest themselves in the new SBC. They call their annual meeting a "general assembly" rather than a convention. They publish a complimentary newsletter, *The Fellowship News*, to inform Baptists about their ministry and missions programs.

Like the Alliance, the CBF is a place where Baptists who do not see themselves as fundamentalists can do ministry together with like-minded moderates. Unlike the Alliance, the CBF tries to cast a wider net, providing a place for disenfranchised Baptists who do not see themselves on the radical edge. Many CBF supporters are people who liked being Southern Baptists in the days when the SBC was more inclusive, and had a mixture of progressive as well as conservative elements. The CBF is has avoided matters of extreme controversy and is genuinely centrist or conservative in its theology and practice. Much of the CBF's work gets done through networking on the old Baptist "society" model, rather than through centralized ownership of institutions.

With the successful launch of CBF in 1991, the SBC Forum, formed by moderate Southern Baptists in 1984 as an alternative to the SBC Pastor's conference, formally dissolved itself in 1991.

CBF elected Cecil Sherman, pastor of Broadway Baptist Church, Fort Worth, Texas, as national coordinator in early 1992, effective March 1st.[246] BCMP's assets were given to CBF in March 1992 and CBF appointed its first missionaries, Charles and Kathie Thomas, who had resigned as FMB missionaries the previous October. Ruschlikon seminary president John David and Jo Ann Hopper were appointed in May 1992 when they resigned as FMB missionaries.

In April 1992, seven SBC agencies who had planned to sponsor exhibits at the CBF Assembly in May canceled those plans after receiving phone calls from Morris Chapman, president-elect of the SBC executive committee.[247] Chapman led an anti-CBF effort which eventually led the 1994 Southern Baptist Convention to refuse any and all CBF Funds. The CBF had been sending financial contributions to specific SBC agencies, particularly the mission boards. All SBC agencies and boards have been directed since 1994 to send back any such contributions.

The Cooperative Baptist Fellowship offered a no-strings attached gift of $100,000 to the Southern Baptist Woman's Missionary Union in 1994 in appreciation for the excellent work the WMU does in missions education. FMB president Rankin urged the WMU to refuse the money. (In 1995, Rankin would send out 11,500 letters criticizing the WMU for producing CBF-related mission material.) The WMU is not an agency of the SBC, but an auxiliary, and thus, not controlled by the SBC. The WMU executive board was not intimidated and voted to accept the gift.[248]

Keith Parks, who retired as FMB president in October 1992, announced the following month that he would assume the position of missions coordinator for CBF. Baptist leaders Jimmy R. Allen, Carolyn Weatherford Crumpler, Grady C. Cothan, Foy D. Valentine, James M. Dunn, W. Randall Lolley, Duke K. McCall, and Darold H. Morgan issued a statement praising Parks for his "courage and integrity," and "affirming his decision to direct the missions program of CBF."[249]

In 1993, CBF adopted a global missions program, devised by Parks, that focuses on "World A" people groups, or ethnic-linguistic groups who have had little access to the gospel, rather than on nation-states or geography.[250] The plan was to avoid duplicating efforts already in place among Southern Baptists. Dr. Parks in particular wanted to send missionaries to the most difficult places, where Baptist mission work is not normally done. CBF had already approved $1.3 million in missions money for Europe in 1993. During 1993, CBF would name a coordinator to help uninsured and under insured Miami-area victims of Hurricane Andrew and send $25,000 to assist with a feeding program for victims of the Midwest floods.

Contributions to CBF have grown rapidly since its organization. In 1991, $4.5 million was received from 391 churches. In 1993, 2,510 individuals contributed directly to CBF, in many cases because their churches would not forward mission offerings to the Fellowship.[251] CBF set a proposed budget of $14,840,000 for the 1998-99 fiscal year. Of this budget, 63% was set aside for Global Missions funding more than 140 career missionaries and persons serving two- to three-year assignments. In 1998, approximately 1,600 churches contributed to the Fellowship's ministry budget.

The 1995 General Assembly meeting in Fort Worth, Texas, adopted the following purpose:

We are a fellowship of Baptist Christians and churches who share a passion for the Great Commission of Jesus Christ and a commitment to Baptist principles of faith and practice. Our mission is to network, empower and mobilize Baptist Christians and churches for effective missions and ministry in the name of Christ.

CBF staff have responded to attempts to discredit the Fellowship in several areas. One common tactic of fundamentalist opponents has been to frighten people by suggesting that the CBF is affiliated with persons and ideas that most centrist Baptists would find disturbing. After some opposition leaders declared the CBF of to be "soft on homosexuality," former Coordinator Cecil Sherman responded by expressing his own views as representative of most CBF participants. His response is summarized in the following points:

1) The Bible teaches homosexuality is a sin;

2) the gay interpreter of the Bible twists the first and traditional meaning of the text;

3) gays can change;

4) local congregations will decide the issue; and

5) we need the spirit of Jesus as we deal with the person who is gay or lesbian.[252]

Many Fellowship members at the 1994 General Assembly wanted to respond in some way to the March 1994 firing of Southwestern Seminary president Russell Dilday. In 1993, the CBF sent $492,037 to the six SBC seminaries, including $164,871 to Southwestern. One motion at the General Assembly suggested that the CBF protest the Dilday firing by excluding all SBC seminaries from all future CBF budgets. Following a healthy debate, the CBF determined to "take the high road" and continued to offer funds to all the seminaries.[253]

Cecil Sherman retired as CBF coordinator in June 1996. The Coordinating Council of the CBF unanimously elected Daniel Vestal, the son of a Southern Baptist evangelist and pastor of Tallowood Baptist Church in Houston since 1991, as the second coordinator of the 5-year-old Fellowship in September 1996. He began his leadership with "a deep conviction God has called me to this place and this task" on December 1, 1996.[254] Thomas S. Boland, a retired Atlanta bank executive, served as interim coordinator after Sherman's retirement and before Vestal began his work as coordinator.

State CBF organizations have grown to the point where coordinators have been elected to assist in CBF work in the various states. States which have elected full-time coordinators include Alabama, Oklahoma, Florida, Georgia, Missouri, Mississippi, South Carolina, Kentucky and Tennessee. Other states have part-time coordinators.[255]

The CBF General Assembly meets annually in different regions of the country. The annual assembly is traditionally Thursday-Saturday during the fourth week in June. The General Assembly sponsors a variety of "breakout sessions" to educate people on a wide variety of issues and interests. The plenary meetings give considerable attention to worship and celebration, and the leadership at the podium is strongly committed to diversity. Responsibilities are very intentionally divided between clergy and laity, men and women.

28. Smyth & Helwys

Smyth & Helwys, Inc. – named after early English Baptist separatists John Smyth and Thomas Helwys – began operation in 1990 to publish books and Sunday School resources for individuals and congregations uncomfortable with the fundamentalist-dominated Southern Baptist Sunday School Board. In 1991, Smyth & Helwys entered into cooperation with Mercer University Press in Macon, Georgia, with Cecil P. Staton, Jr. becoming publisher of both publishing houses and president of Smyth and Helwys.[256]

Smyth & Helwys earned high marks in a 1993 study. Its Sunday School curriculum, *Formations*, was rated fifth best among 42 programs studied; Baptist Sunday School Board literature was rated 11th.[257] Today, more than 2,000 churches in 48 states and several foreign use *Formations* resources for all ages. Although the primary market for this literature is moderate Baptist churches, Smyth and Helwys has no formal tie to CBF, the Alliance of Baptists or any other denominational group.

In 1993, Smyth & Helwys introduced its first Vacation Bible School resource, A *Heart for Missions*. Two additional VBS resources have been produced including *Celebrate Freedom*, a Baptist distinctives VBS in 1998. In 1999, Smyth & Helwys published, in cooperation with Habitat for Humanity International, a new VBS resource, *Under Construction*.

Smyth & Helwys has published 200 books since 1991 and currently publishes approximately 40 new books annually. Publisher Cecil Staton announced in 1994 plans for a new 30 volume Bible commentary series. The first volumes will premier in 1999; the project will take approximately 10 years to complete.

In 1996, Smyth & Helwys launched the first Baptist service on the World Wide Web www.helwys.com. Baptistnet was also launched as a gathering place on the Web for Baptists worldwide www.helwys.com/baptistnet.html.

As noted earlier, Smyth & Helwys assumed management of BAPTISTS TODAY in October 1998. The newspaper was moved from its Decatur, Ga., offices to Macon.

29. Whisitt Baptist Heritage Society

There is an old maxim that says, "Those who do not learn from history are doomed to repeat it." But another old maxim reminds us that "history is written by the winners." Having lost the SBC to the takeover faction, Baptist moderates were concerned to establish a truthful and academically reliable repository of Baptist history. This was especially important to Baptist leaders who felt that the fundamentalist takeover faction had mis-repre-sented denominational history to suit their own ends. Moderate Baptists voted to form a new Baptist "heritage" society, the Walter H. Whisitt Baptist Heritage Society, in October 1992 during a meeting in Macon, Georgia. Walter Whisitt was forced to resign from Southern Seminary in 1898 after he wrote an article op-posing the view that Baptists can trace their roots in a "trail of blood" to John the Baptist. Calling for a more honest approach to Baptist history, Whisitt argued that Baptists emerged in the early 17th century.

The society publishes *The Whitsitt Journal.*

30. 1993 Southern Baptist Convention: Houston

Messengers at the 1993 SBC sought to chastize President Bill Clinton and Vice President Al Gore for their positions on abor-tion and homosexuals in the military. At least 18 of the more than 40 resolutions blasted the two fellow Southern Baptists. Some messengers wanted to refuse voting privileges for mes-sengers from Immanuel Baptist Church in Little Rock, Arkansas, where Clinton still keeps his membership. The ten messengers were required to defend themselves before the credentials com-mittee before being seated because of a 1992 SBC decision re-fusing Convention membership to any church which endorses or sanctions a homosexual lifestyle. The messengers from Immanuel Baptist had to explain that they were not account-able for the political and governing decisions of their famous member. A motion was also introduced to expel the church from the SBC.[258] These attempts to chastize the President by way of refusing to accept his church failed, but set the tone for that year's convention.

Also during the 1993 Convention an undated offset, "Under-standing the Controversy" by Southeastern Seminary president Paige Patterson, was passed out at the Southeastern display booth.[259] Patterson outlined the controversy by dividing the theological schools of thought into orthodoxy; neo-orthodoxy, which he said was "really neo-liberalism;" and classical liberalism. Patterson argued that schools reflecting orthodoxy include Mid-America Baptist Theological Seminary, The Criswell College, Luther Rice Seminary, and Southeastern Seminary. Representative orthodox Baptists include W. A. Criswell, Adrian Rogers, Charles Stanley, and Paul Pressler.

Patterson said neo-orthodox prefer the title "conservatives," "moderates, or "denominational loyalists." Neo-orthodox schools include Baylor University and Midwestern Seminary. Representative Baptists include Cecil Sherman, Russell Dilday, Milton Ferguson, and "most Baptist state paper editors." Dilday responded with wry humor by saying this was "just another Paigerism."[260] Ferguson issued a "Statement to all Southern Baptists" saying he was "grieved by the gross misrepresentations" of his theological convictions.

Schools representing the classical liberal position were said to be Stetson University, Mercer University, Wake Forest University and the University of Richmond. Patterson said the distribution of the offset was not authorized.

The Houston Convention also approved a controversial report on Freemasonry presented by the HMB after a 2-year, $110,000 study. James Larry Holly, a Beaumont, Texas physician, had introduced a resolution at the 1991 SBC to condemn Freemasonry. Holly earlier took credit for helping force the early retirement of Sunday School Board president Lloyd Elder.[261] The HMB declined to conduct a study after the resolution was forwarded to the agency, since that agency had responded to a similar resolution in 1985. However, messengers to the 1992 SBC directed the HMB to conduct the study and bring a report to the 1993 Convention.

The HMB report to the Houston convention listed eight points which it stated were "not compatible with Christianity or Southern Baptist doctrine," but stopped short of condemning Freemasonry. The report concluded that membership in the Masonic fraternity is a personal matter for individuals and local churches to decide, not the SBC.

Baptist critics took Freemasonry to task over several issues, including the misuse of religious language and teachings or assumptions incompatible with Christianity. One such criticism concerned the use of the title, "Worshipful Master." Masons responded that "worshipful" means "honorable or respected." For example, the mayor of London, England is referred to as "Worshipful Lord Mayor." English reformer John Wyclif (1324-1384) translated Exodus 20:12, "Thou shalt worship thy father and thy mother, that thou be long lived upon earth."[262] Masons explained that the so-called "bloody oaths" are symbolic and remind the Mason of the evils of religious and political tyranny. The Masonic term "light" was taken by some Baptist critics as a reference to salvation. Fundamentalists did not trust Masonic insistence that the term referred to knowledge or truth. Masons pointed to the fact that the motto of the *Baltimore Sun* is "Light for all," which is hardly a reference to salvation. The motto of Yale University is "LUX," a Latin word for "light." Few Masons knew what the HMB report was referring to when it condemned Freemasonry for the "heresy of universalism," as they insist the fraternity is not a religion and therefore offers no teaching on salvation.

Defenders of Masonic membership pointed out that many devout Southern Baptist leaders of long-standing positive influence had been Masons. Famous Southern Baptist Masons have included George W. Truett, long-time pastor of First Baptist Church, Dallas, Texas; Herschell H. Hobbs, one of the most popular and respected Southern Baptist pastors, theologians and leaders; and Bernard W. Spilman, who founded the Ridgecrest Baptist Assembly near Black Mountain, N.C.

Gary Leazer, a member of the Interfaith Witness Department staff since February 1979, had supervised the committee which conducted the original study on Freemasonry. He was forced to resign from the Home Mission Board in October 1993 after he gave a speech to a Masonic group to explain the meaning of the vote at the Houston SBC. Even though his job description permitted him to speak to non-SBC groups to explain Southern Baptist theology and polity, Leazer was accused of "gross insubordination" for speaking at the Masonic meeting.

31. 1994 Southern Baptist Convention: Orlando

The election of a new president, concern about the growth of CBF, and the angry reaction to the firing of popular Southwestern Seminary president Russell Dilday.

At the 1994 Southern Baptist Convention in Orlando, Jim Henry, pastor of First Baptist Church, Orlando, was elected SBC President, defeating Fred Wolfe, 9,876-8,023. This was an un-expected development for the takeover faction. Fred Wolfe had been hand-picked by the takeover coalition and nominated by fundamentalist luminary Charles Stanley. After Henry announced he would be a candidate for SBC president, leading fundamentalists, including Paul Pressler, Paige Patterson, Adrian Rogers, Charles Stanley, Bailey Smith, and at least ten others held a private meeting in Atlanta in April to discuss the Henry candidacy and the Dilday firing.[263]

Although not the handpicked candidate, and seen by some as a reconciler, Henry said he would appoint only inerrantists who affirm both the Baptist Faith and Message and the Peace Committee report.[264] After the election, Henry and Wolfe attended a joint victory celebration, planned two days earlier regardless of who was elected.

A motion to appoint a committee to investigate Dilday's firing was defeated.

By 1994 the fledgling Cooperative Baptist Fellowship was demonstrating greater strength than many SBC leaders had expected. Fundamentalists did not want to give any further legitimacy to the movement by accepting funds from the organization. Convention messengers passed a motion, 4,730 to 3,342, directing SBC agencies and institutions to decline CBF funds. Receipts forwarded to SBC causes through the CBF in 1991-1993 were:

1991	$2,648,691
1992	$3,275,141
1993	$2,715,050

Most of the receipts had been specifically designated to the two mission boards. In 1993 alone, the Foreign Mission Board received $1.6 million and the Home Mission Board $434,000.[265] The SBC Executive Committee, which had received less than $30 from the CBF in the three years (1991-1993), led to move to reject CBF money.

Since CBF funds could no longer be forwarded directly to SBC agencies, CBF officers eliminated two giving plans which forwarded percentages to SBC agencies and institutions.[266]

Oddly enough, while severing all ties with fellow Southern Baptists in the CBF, the SBC passed a resolution affirming dialogue with Roman Catholics. Marv Knox, editor of Kentucky Baptists' *Western Recorder*, called these decisions "ironic."[267] Presnall H. Wood, editor of *The Baptist Standard*, says the vote "means the Southern Baptist Convention has come dangerously close to telling individuals in local churches how they must give to be a loyal Southern Baptist."[268]

In August 1994, in response to the SBC directive, Home Mission Board directors voted to stop receiving funds from CBF. At the same meeting, directors eliminated 22 staff positions and suspended funding for 3 others, due to insufficient finances.[269] In September 1994, the SBC Executive Committee asked state conventions to cut all CBF ties. Since state conventions are autonomous, the Executive Committee could only request such an action.

32. SBC Controversy Moves to States

"The big difference between Texas Baptists and Southern Baptists has been we let everybody play." — Charles Wade, pastor of the First

Baptist Church, Arlington, Texas, and president of the Baptist General Convention of Texas.

As expected, the SBC controversy has moved to the state convention level as moderates attempt to hold and fundamentalists attempt to take over leadership of the state conventions. At first, elections of state convention presidents swung back and forth as the two groups vied for their candidates. Increasingly, fundamentalists began winning an increasing number of elections on the state level.

In June 1994, the Home Mission Board (HMB) executive committee voted to consider changing ways it relates to state conventions which channel funds through their offices to the CBF. Twelve states allow such funding. Baptist State Convention of North Carolina executive Roy Smith, responded, "The 'C' in CP [Cooperative Program] stands for cooperation, not control." In 1993, North Carolina Baptists sent more than $5.3 million to the HMB and received $475,000 in grants from the HMB. Smith said, "We will continue home missions in North Carolina, with or without the Home Mission Board."[270]

Funding of CBF has become an issue in several other states. The Baptist General Association of Virginia allows churches to select one of three "tracks" for the distribution of their mission funds; one track forwards funds to the CBF.[271] The Baptist General Convention of Texas broadened the definition of Cooperative Program gifts and approved a giving plan which allowed Texas Baptists to support a variety of worldwide Baptist causes, including CBF.[272]

In 1993, Southern Baptist Conservatives of Virginia (SBCV) organized in opposition to the more moderate Baptist General Association of Virginia (BGAV). A spokesman for the SBCV said its "main role is to maintain strong loyalty to the Southern Baptist Convention."[273] In September 1994, newly elected SBCV president, Bob Melvin, pastor of Spotswood Baptist Church in Fredericksburg, dismissed speculation the SBCV would separate from the BGAV to form a new state Baptist association affiliated with the SBC. However, in September 1996, the SBCV voted to form their own state convention — the first such action in the history of the SBC.[274]

Fundamentalists, including a number of SBC Executive Committee members and other "like-minded people," met in Nashville, Tenn., on February 23-24, 1994, to "discuss developments in various state conventions." Reflecting fundamentalists distrust of state Baptist papers, a state newspaper editor was asked to leave the meeting by SBC Executive Committee member T. C. Pinckney of Virginia, a leader of the Southern Baptist Conservatives of Virginia.[275]

Texas fundamentalist Walter Carpenter filed a charter for the "Texas Baptist Convention, Inc." in 1994 "should the need arise for a new convention."[276] After the Texas Baptist state convention in October 1994, fundamentalists organized the Texas Conservative Baptist Fellowship, "a loose-knit organization to promote fundamentalist causes."[277]

Fundamentalists announced Southern Baptists of Texas will become a separate state convention in November 1998. Paige Patterson gave a keynote address at a statewide rally of the Southern Baptists of Texas in April 1998. Texas will be the second state to have two separate state conventions.[278]

Alabama fundamentalists formed Southern Baptist Conservatives of Alabama in 1997 and elected a steering committee in April 1998. Interim moderator Steve Loggins said, "We don't want to take over, just be heard..."[279]

Fundamentalists in Missouri formed Project 1000, a statewide effort to encourage fundamentalist Baptists to participate as messengers at the annual Missouri Baptist Convention meeting. They held a strategy meeting in Kansas City with Southeastern Seminary president (and now SBC president) Paige Patterson in April 1998.[280]

Many state convention leaders have become more discriminatory about people they invite to participate in state convention activities. Invitations to individuals seen as too friendly toward CBF have been withdrawn. Gary Cook, pastor of First Baptist Church, Lawton, Okla., and a former vice president of the Sunday School Board (now LifeWay Christian Resources) was replaced on the Oklahoma state convention's strategic planning committee because he served as moderator of a discussion group at a state CBF meeting.[281]

The fundamentalist/moderate controversy is no longer a "live issue" on the national level. The takeover faction is now firmly in control of the Southern Baptist Convention institutions, and the moderates have organized new national organizations for mission, ministry and fellowship. But the struggle for political control has merely moved into the state conventions.

The controversy has merely moved into the state conventions.

33. 1995 Convention Approves Restructuring of SBC

The SBC Executive Committee announced and recommended approval of the Brister Report (named after Mark Brister, chair of the 7-member Program and Structure Study Committee) to eliminate or merge a number of SBC agencies and commissions. The report called for the reduction of the number of agencies and commissions from 19 to 12.

Most significant of the proposals was the merger of the Home Mission Board, Radio and Television Commission and the Brotherhood Commission into the North American Mission Board to be headquartered in Alpharetta, a suburb in far north Atlanta.

The proposal called for changing the names of the Foreign Mission Board to the International Mission Board, and the Christian Life Commission to the Ethics and Religious Liberty Commission. It also called for the elimination of the SBC Historical Commission with responsibility for the SBC's historical library and archives given to the presidents of the six SBC seminaries. The elimination of the Historical Commission aroused a great deal of concern.

A staff member for Lynn May of the SBC Historical Commission read a statement from May, "I cannot and will not support a recommendation for dismantling the Historical Commission and reassigning of some of its program assignments and functions to other agencies."[282] State Baptist historians also opposed dissolving the SBC Historical Commission. But, as one staff member of the North American Mission Board reportedly would say later, "We have no history; we are here to make history."

Stewardship Commission president Ronald E. Chandler expressed his conviction dissolving the commission "is not in the best interest of the Southern Baptist Convention."[283] Brotherhood Commission trustees unanimously adopted a statement saying, "We do not embrace or support the recommendation in its current form."[284]

Messengers at the 1995 SBC adopted the Brister Report restructuring the SBC. In other action, the SBC overwhelmingly adopted a resolution renouncing its racist past as it celebrated its Sesquicentennial in Atlanta.

34. Woman's Missionary Union

The national WMU has fallen out of favor with the powers-that-be in Nashville because they extended their missionary educational services to "other" Southern Baptists, namely the missionary-sending organization known as the Cooperative Baptist Fellowship.

Whereas the Baptist Sunday School Board for years has profitably produced material for non-SBC denominations. — Harold Shirley, Rock Hill, S.C.[285]

Woman's Missionary Union, the driving force behind the Annie Armstrong and Lottie Moon missions offerings, has drawn the ire of current SBC leadership because of their cooperation with the CBF. This has proved to be a difficult problem for the fundamentalist leadership, because the WMU is an "auxiliary" of the SBC. They elect their own directors and so cannot be "controlled" by the takeover faction.

In 1992 the WMU had decided to produce and distribute information regarding the mission activities of the CBF, in addition to their continuing promotion of SBC missions. In January of 1995 John Jackson, the Chairman of the Board of Trustees for the Foreign Mission Board, likened the WMU's stance to that of an adulterous woman who says to the SBC, "I know we have had such a good working relationship, but I know that you won't mind if I bring [another man] into our bed."[286]

In September 1995, Foreign Mission Board president Rankin mailed a letter to 40,000 pastors and WMU directors urging them to pray that the national WMU would change its mind about producing materials for CBF. According to David Button at the FMB, it cost about $11,500 for the mailing. WMU Executive Director Dellanna O'Brien called the letter "inflammatory, misleading and divisive," saying the WMU is responding to requests from churches requesting information about what CBF is doing in missions."[287] O'Brien also criticized the "absence of a clear statement about WMU's proposed involvement" in SBC missions in the 1995 restructuring proposal.[288]

Many people, both moderate and fundamentalist, believe the SBC leadership will address their problem with the WMU in some way in the future. James C. Hefley, a well-known fundamentalist author, states two "possible outcome[s]," should SBC fundamentalists attempt to diminish the influence of the WMU in Southern Baptist life. First, the SBC may "revoke its auxiliary relationship with the national WMU and establish a new agency for women's ministries within the SBC structure." Second, the SBC may "request another agency (perhaps the Sunday School Board) to prepare materials for missionary education and women's ministries."[289]

The second possible outcome seems more likely. The SBC leadership will slowly increase the missions and women's emphases of the Sunday School Board/LifeWay Christian Resources, North American Mission Board, and the seminaries, while ignoring the WMU.

35. 1996 SBC in New Orleans targets Disney, Reorganizes Agencies

Meeting in New Orleans, SBC messengers elected Tom Elliff, Bailey Smith's brother-in-law, as president. He was the choice of about 80 fundamentalist leaders who met in Atlanta in November 1995, hoping to avoid the awkward showdown that resulted in Jim Henry's election as SBC president in 1994. One fundamentalist called Jim Henry's nominees "weak."[290] Associated Baptist Press reported that Elliff and Paige Patterson emerged as the group's favorites at the November meeting, with Elliff drawing six more votes than Patterson in a secret ballot. Patterson withdrew his name to give Elliff the nod (Patterson's turn would come in 1998 after Elliff served the customary two terms.).[291] During the 1996 Convention, Elliff called on Southern Baptists who do not subscribe to his version of inerrancy to "repent."[292]

Messengers passed a non-binding resolution on the Disney Company urging members to "give serious and prayerful reconsideration" before purchasing Disney products. Messengers said Disney's practice of providing insurance for same-sex partners of employees was offensive, as was permitting homosexual and lesbian theme nights.[293]

Messengers also approved a massive "Covenant for a New Century" restructuring plan to reduce the number of convention agencies from 19 to 12.

Baptist leaders admitted later they "were frankly caught off guard" by the fury unleashed by a resolution passed at the convention calling on Southern Baptists to "direct our energies and resources toward the proclamation of the gospel to the Jewish people." Jewish leaders accused Southern Baptists of "singling out Jews as a target for conversions" and of insulting the Jewish people. The response, SBC leaders said, was "reminiscent of the backlash felt in 1980 after a widely publicized remark by SBC President Bailey Smith that God `does not hear the prayers of a Jew'."[294]

36. 1997 Convention Again Targets The Disney Company

"Most of the people who attended the [1997] annual meeting of the Southern Baptist Convention represented the far, far, far right wing of the denomination. That is why the meeting was so `peaceful,' so agreeable. Few opposing voices were present." — Pat Anderson, Coordinator, Florida Cooperative Baptist Fellowship.[295]

While avoiding the word "boycott," the SBC followed up on a 1996 SBC resolution calling for a boycott if Disney continued its "anti-Christian and anti-family trends." The 1997 resolution encouraged Southern Baptists "to refrain from patronizing The Disney Company and any of its related companies."[296]

37. 1998 Convention, Salt Lake City, Elects Patterson President

To my way of thinking, there's not room in Baptist life for all viewpoints.
— Paige Patterson

Without opposition, Southeastern Seminary president Paige Patterson, was elected President of the Southern Baptist Convention by acclamation at the 1998 Southern Baptist Convention in Salt Lake City. Patterson is recognized as launching the theological and political takeover that turned the SBC sharply to the right. Moderate Southern Baptists stopped nominating candidates for the office of SBC president after 1990.

Patterson announced his emphasis as president would be evangelism and church planting. His baptism goal for 2000, he said, is one million people — 500,000 baptisms in the United States and 500,000 overseas. Baptisms in the United States numbered 412,000 in 1997, 293,100 overseas.[297] Overseas baptisms have traditionally not been counted in SBC figures since overseas churches are not part of the Southern Baptist Convention.

Patterson said fundamentalists are simply doing what the Bible says. Those who think otherwise aren't welcome in the SBC tent. "To my way of thinking, there's not room in Baptist life for all viewpoints."[298]

Falwell Attends SBC as Messenger for First Time

We keep hoping that Uncle Jerry will come our way. — Paige Patterson in a 1994 Virginia speech.[299]

I think he [Jerry Falwell] fits right in with the SBC in terms of theology. — Doyle Chauncey, executive director, Southern Baptist Conservatives of Virginia.[300]

Well-known fundamentalist Jerry Falwell, who had spoken at the SBC Pastors' Conference, in SBC churches and at other SBC functions, registered for the first time as a voting messenger at the Southern Baptist Convention in Salt Lake City. Falwell and seven other members of Thomas Road Baptist Church in Lynchburg, Va., registered one year after the church joined with a new state convention formed by fundamentalists in Virginia. Thomas Road Baptist Church contributed $10,000 to SBC causes in 1997.[301] Falwell said his church still has not abandoned the Baptist Bible Fellowship, which was formed in 1950 by dissatisfied followers of J. Frank Norris's World Baptist Fellowship.

Falwell announced Liberty University is training 1,000 pastors and he plans to work with Patterson to start "a lot of new Southern Baptist churches."[302] Falwell also spoke at the Sunday School Board's National Conference for Church Leadership at Ridgecrest (N.C.) Conference Center in June 1998. Some Southern Baptists questioned the choice of Falwell as a speaker, citing Falwell's speech at Southeastern Seminary in March 1997 when he said, "I thank God that one day, Virginia — the most liberal of all

Baptist states in the nation — and North Carolina — who has the dubious distinction of being No. 2 worst — will have the best because of Southeastern producing the pastors, the mentors, the leaders who will replace the duds with good Bible-teaching and Bible-preaching pulpits."[303] In 1997, Patterson called Falwell his "mentor of worldwide rabble-rousing."[304]

Toby A. Druin, editor of the *Baptist Standard*, raised the question, "Paige Patterson may be the new president, but look to Falwell to begin to get the spotlight. And if Falwell is going to be the spokesman, why not president [of the SBC], too?"[305]

Even the fundamentalist newspaper, *The Sword of the Lord*, asked the question: "Will Dr. Falwell Be SBC President?" Its response, "That question is already being bantered around inside the SBC. It is of course hard to predict what will happen from one day to the next. But it is certainly plausible and quite likely to occur sometime in the not-too-distant future!"[306] This would be significant because Falwell's well known media status as the very symbol of aggressive right wing political activism anointed with fundamentalist conviction. Even more than he does now, Falwell would come to represent the meaning of the name: Southern Baptist.

SBC Adopts New Statement on the Family

One of the most significant goals of the fundamentalist faction has been to promote a more traditional approach to family relationships—an approach that affirms a divinely ordained authority of the husband over his wife. The 1998 Southern Baptist Convention approved a new article on the family as an amendment to the 35 year old *Baptist Faith and Message*. Adoption of the article marks the first time the *Baptist Faith and Message* has been changed since its adoption in 1963.

Members of the committee appointed by SBC president Tom Elliff to develop the article said its purpose was to "give a clear call to biblical principles of family life." However, a statement in the article that "A wife is to submit herself graciously" to her husband drew two amendments, both of which failed in separate votes by show of ballots. One failed amendment suggested that "Both husband and wife are to submit graciously to each other as servant leaders in the home, even as the church willingly submits to the lordship of Christ." The author of the failed amendment, Tim Owings, First Baptist Church, Augusta, Ga., said he based his amendment on Ephesians 5:21, which states, "Submit to one another out of reverence for Christ." The committee chose to emphasize Ephesians 5:22, emphasizing the wife's duty to her husband.[307]

Mark Wingfield, of Kentucky's *Western Recorder*, wrote in an editorial, "Individual Southern Baptists have been left scrambling to explain to co-workers, neighbors and family members what this doctrinal statement really means and how it came to be. Sadly, this has not increased opportunities for a positive gospel witness but has raised more suspicion in many minds about the unity of the church and the validity of the essential message."[308]

Tinkering with the Baptist Faith and Message statement continued to be a favorite fundamentalist pre-occupation in the 1999 Southern Baptist Convention in Atlanta. Such tinkering is especially chilling in light of Paige Patterson's previously mentioned comment that

"...there's not room in Baptist life for all viewpoints." At the Atlanta meeting the convention voted to appoint a committee to review the Baptist Faith and Message Statement. Speaking in favor of the motion one messenger said, "We need a statement of faith that is clear and unambiguous."[309] Such comment suggests that the SBC will seek to make the traditional Southern Baptist Confession of faith more "unambiguously" fundamentalist.

As the Baptist Faith and Message statement has already been used to some degree as a creedal text to enforce doctrinal uniformity, Baptists can be sure it will be used that way even more stringently as it is altered to reflect fundamentalist sensibilities. In all likelihood, those who wish to participate in denominational life will have less and less freedom to think differently on even the finest points of belief. It is also possible that the denomination will suffer further fractures as the fundamentalists try to outdo each other in their orthodoxies.

Other Decisions

Messengers approved a name change for the Baptist Sunday School Board. The new name is LifeWay Christian Resources of the Southern Baptist Convention. Messengers also approved reducing the annual Convention meetings from three days to two days beginning in 1999.

Three messengers asked the Executive Committee to consider changing the location of the SBC's 2000 annual meeting from Orlando to another city in light of Southern Baptists' boycott of the Walt Disney Co. Breaking agreements already in place with Orlando could cost the SBC as much as $300,000. The motions were referred to the Executive Committee for action, and eventually the SBC decided to honor their agreements with Orlando.

Sermon Highlights

James G. Merritt, pastor of First Baptist Church, Snellville, Ga., preached the convention sermon. He warned that schools, churches and denominations are "like a car out of line — without a firm hand on the wheel they will always drift. And they never veer to the right; they always veer to the left." He added, "The battle for the soul of our denomination, our colleges and seminaries, our churches, even the Bible itself, will never be over."[310] Merritt warned that "There may be a cease fire, but ...we can never let our guard down." He warned about "spiritual crocodiles that line the banks of the river of Christianity" and "stealth liberals who fly in under spiritual radar" to steal colleges, seminaries, churches and denominations — obvious references to moderates.[311]

SBC president Tom Elliff thanked those who had "rescued our ship from peril" during "the conservative resurgence" of the past 20 years. Elliff spoke of the "thunder that shook off the barnacles of parasitic unions, conferences and fellowships ...no matter how Baptist or Cooperative (yea, capital `C') they might have deemed themselves ...." Toby A. Druin, in an editorial in the *Baptist Standard*, said, "I can't imagine one Southern Baptist calling another a `barnacle' or `parasite'."[312]

38. Editorial: "Who is the Enemy?"

In an editorial in the October 21, 1993 issue of Virginia's *Religious Herald*, Michael Clingenpeel, wrote these words which provide excellent insight into the nature of fundamentalism:

> What bothers me most these days is the cavalier manner in which some Christians label as enemies other Christians with whom they have practical and theological differences... One of the truths I have learned about enemies is that some people cannot live without them. Remove an enemy and they immediately look for and latch onto another. Our nation, denomination and churches are full of people who function only when crusading against something. Another thing I've learned is that people can designate you as their enemy and almost nothing you do can convince them to alter their opinion of you... As far as I can tell, the Pharisees were the only group in the Gospels who consistently asked the question, "Who is my enemy?" And always they arrived at one answer — Jesus.
>
> Jesus, on the other hand, almost never divided people into enemies and friends. He treated as friends people who logically were adversaries of his ministry and standard of righteousness — men and women such as tax collectors, prostitutes and Samaritans. He taught his disciples to ask,"Who is my neighbor?" instead of "Who is my enemy?"
>
> One final thing I've learned. Beware of any Christian group that defines itself more by who it opposes than by who it affirms. The act of defining an enemy is often prejudicial and judgmental. Almost always it leads to angry attitudes and destructive actions...

39. Takeover Not Over

Affirming inerrancy is only the first step in the SBC takeover, according to Alan Day, pastor of the First Baptist Church, Edmond, Oklahoma. In a March 10, 1998 sermon to students and faculty at Southern Baptist Theological Seminary in Louisville, Ky., Day said,

> I'm disturbed that — after the 'Battle for the Bible,' after the war to make our denomination safe for orthodoxy, after we've won the right to use the words 'inerrant' and 'infallible' in polite company, ...that nevertheless across our convention, even in the pulpits of some who ballyhoo inerrancy and infallibility and orthodoxy, we see being employed a secular methodology, a secular eccelesiology and a preaching that very little oftentimes resembles the faith once for all delivered to the saints.

Day continued, "There must be reform of our preaching or the gains of the past 20 years will be lost."[313] At a meeting of Calvinist Southern Baptists, Mark Dever, pastor of Capitol Hill Baptist Church in Washington, said affirming the inerrancy of the Bible is not enough. He said the next necessary step in reforming the church is a call to make expository preaching the norm for all true men of God.[314]

These comments by Day and Dever make it clear that the takeover is not over. For fundamentalists, much more must be done to consolidate the victories of the past 20 years. Part of the essence of fundamentalism is the drive to make everyone else over in their image. So, in the struggle to determine who is more truly orthodox there will always be new tests people must pass in order to belong. As the Pharisees demonstrated in Jesus' day, the list of laws and new standards to live up to can be almost endless. It is possible that the takeover faction will fragment the SBC into even smaller, exclusivistic enclaves. Beyond all that, there are still states to conquer. There are still mainstream Baptists to intimidate and convert.

40. Conclusions

In presenting some of the main events involved in the takeover
in the Southern Baptist Convention, this short history has gradually built a case to establish the following as a fact:

**The Southern Baptist Convention has been taken over by a highly
organized group of fundamentalists who, speaking for only a
minority of the Southern Baptist constituency, have remolded
the SBC in defiance of some of the most cherished features of
the historic Baptist identity.**

What are the consequences of this fundamentalist coup? One
tragedy of the takeover has been the destruction of trust. The
Southern Baptist Convention is a loose-knit structure that could
never have worked without firm foundations of trust. Much of
that has now been washed away by wave after wave of accusa-
tion — accusations laced with large doses of ignorance and mis-
information about Baptist identity and Southern Baptist history–
accusations designed to exaggerate differences and bring faithful Christian servants into disrepute.

The evidence contained in this booklet demonstrates that:

1) The takeover of the Southern Baptist Convention has changed
the character of the denomination from one of openness to
one of restricted thought, from one of spiritual liberty to one
of tyranny.

2) The political campaign to gain control of the denomination
was carried out in a sinful and mean-spirited fashion, using
innuendo, glittering generalities and exaggerations to achieve
the ends of power.

3) The resulting changes have defied the perfect will and purpose of God, while hurting fellow believers and dishonoring
the noble tradition of what it means to be Baptist.

The support provided to and energy from such groups as the
CBF, the Alliance of Baptists and Texas Baptists Committed, shows

quite clearly that the takeover faction never really spoke for all "Bible believing" Baptists. Many good and well-intentioned conservatives have been misled into believing that they voted to "save the SBC" for truth, when in reality they placed the resources of our great denomination in the hands of mean-spirited power-mongers.

Fundamentalists have succeeded in their takeover of the national Convention. They have demonstrated by their past behavior that they will act ruthlessly to preserve their new place in the denomination. They will seek to prevent all who oppose their efforts from exercising their rights as Baptists. They have shown that they are willing to act in closed-door meetings and they determine outcomes for a "democratic denomination" by secret caucuses of the trusted few.[315]

To react wisely and faithfully in face of the takeover, we must read widely, ask hard questions, and courageously speak without being intimidated. This booklet is intended to stimulate that process.

Baptists who are uneasy with the tactics and opinions of the takeover group should seek out the intellectual and spiritual fellowship of moderates in their area. CBF groups have organized in many states for fellowship, as have fundamentalist groups. CBF is a grass-roots movement which is growing from the local level up. That's the Baptist way. Texas Baptists Committed continues to be a significant voice for moderate Texas Baptists.[316] The Baptists Committed model is being started in other states. For those who are looking for a slightly more progressive approach, the Alliance of Baptists are well organized in several of the Southeastern coastal states.

In conclusion, a word to those Southern Baptists who know and care about what it means to be a Baptist: *Freedom is your birthright!* "You were called to freedom" (Gal. 5:13). But how should you use your freedom? Is it right to enjoy the fruit of freedom without shouldering the responsibilities of freedom? It is easier by far to ignore the events described in this booklet, and avoid the pain of confrontation, but whenever we fail to exercise our freedom, whenever we refuse to defend our freedom, freedom slips away.

Selected, annotated Bibliography

Those who wish to read in more detail about the fundamentalist takeover of the Southern Baptist Convention will find more information in the following books:

Baugh, John G. *The Battle for Baptist Integrity.* Austin, Texas: Battle for Baptist Integrity Inc., 1995. (The highly readable observations of a longtime involved Southern Baptist layman.)

Cothen, Grady C. *What Happened to the Southern Baptist Convention? A Memoir of the Controversy.* Macon, GA: Smyth and Helwys Publishing Inc., 1993.

Furguson, Robert U. *Amidst Babel, Speak Truth: Reflections on the Southern Baptist Struggle.* Macon GA: Smyth & Helways Publishing Company, 1993. (Articles on various aspects of the controversy, written by a variety of moderate scholars.)

Humphreys, Fisher, Editor. *The Controversy in the Southern Baptist Convention: A Special Issue of the Theological Educator.* New Orleans Baptist Theological Seminary, 1985. (A compendium of articles and interviews by persons on differing sides of the conflict.)

Humphreys, Fisher, Editor. *Polarities in the Southern Baptist Convention: A Special Issue of the Theological Educator.* New Orleans Baptist Theological Seminary, 1988. (A compendium of more articles and interviews with major personalities on different sides of the controversy.)

Leonard, Bil J. *God's Last and Only Hope: The Fragmentation of the Southern Baptist Convention.* Grand Rapids, Mich.: Eerdman's Publishing Company, 1990.

Robison, James B., Editor. *The Unfettered Word: Confronting the Authority–Innerancy Question.* Macon, GA: Smyth and Helwys Publishing Company, 1994. (Various articles on the issue of Biblical authority and Biblical innerancy.)

Shurden, Walter B. and **Randy Sheply**, Editors. *Going for the Jugular: A documentary History of the SBC Holy War.* Macon, GA:

Mercer University Press, 1996. (A useful chronology of the controversy, along with the publication of articles dealing with the events of the controversy as they occurred.)

Shurden, Walter B., Editor. *The Struggle for the Soul of the* SBC: *Moderate Responses to the Fundamentalist Movement.* Macon, GA: Mercer University Press, 1993. (Moderate leaders tell their stories about the moderate political response to the fundamentalist takeover, and the creation of new Baptist communities in the light of the takeover's final victories.)

Shurden, Walter B. *Not a Silent People: Controversies that Have Shaped Southern Baptists.* Macon, GA: Smyth & Helwys Publishing Company, 1995. (A historical overview of several controversies that have shaped Baptist life, with the story of the fundamentalist takeover added at the end.)

Notes

1. SBC TODAY, July 1990, p. 8.
2. J. M. Carroll, "*The Trail of Blood*" ... *Following the Christians Down Through the Centuries. . . . or The History of Baptist Churches From the Time of Christ, Their Founder, to the Present Day* (Lexington, Kentucky: Ashland Avenue Baptist Church, 1975).
3. Smyth and Helwys, the moderate Baptist publishing house in Macon, Georgia, was named after these two early Baptist dissenters.
4. Henry C. Vedder, *A Short History of the Baptists* (Valley Forge, Penn.: Judson Press, 1907), pp. 262-63.
5. Robert A. Baker, *The Southern Baptist Convention and Its People* (Nashville: Broadman Press, 1974), p. 66.
6. Ibid, p. 67.
7. From *A Declaration of Rights* adopted by the Virginia Convention of 1776, section sixteen, quoted in Robert A. Baker, *A Baptist Source Book* (Nash-

ville: Broadman Press, 1966), pp. 34-35. The statement was originally written by Baptist George Mason. James Madison amended the statement to substitute "free exercise of religion" for "toleration."
8. Baker, *A Baptist Source Book*, p. 40.
9. Ibid, p. 116.
10. The lectures, delivered at Southeastern Baptist Theological Seminary in Wake Forest, North Carolina, are "The Southern Baptist Synthesis: Is It Cracking?" and "The Inerrancy Debate: A Comparative Study of Southern Baptist Controversies." They are published together in *Baptist History and Heritage*, April 1981, pp. 2-19.
11. Walter B. Shurden, "The Southern Baptist Synthesis: Is It Cracking?" *Baptist History and Heritage*, April 1981, pp. 7, 8.
12. H. Leon McBeth, *The Baptist Heritage*

(Nashville: Broadman Press, 1987), p. 685.

13. SBC TODAY, April 1988, p. 4.

14. Leon McBeth, "Fundamentalism in the Southern Baptist Convention in Recent Years," *Review and Expositor*, Winter 1982, pp. 86, 87. In a telephone conversation of December 29, 1988 with Rob James, McBeth stood by what he had said in this 1982 article.

15. George M. Marsden in Norman J. Cohen, ed., *The Fundamentalist Phenomenon: A View from Within; A Response from Without* (Grand Rapids: William B. Eerdmans Publishing Company 1990), p. 22.

16. Nancy Ammerman, *Bible Believers: Fundamentalism in the Modern World* (New Brunswick: Rutgers University Press, 1987), p. 8.

17. Bruce L. Shelley, "Fundamentalism," *The New International Dictionary of the Christian Church*, J.D. Douglas, gen. ed. (Grand Rapids: Zondervan Publishing House, 1974), p. 396.

18. See Jerry Falwell, "An Agenda for the 1980s," and Grant Wacker, "Searching for Norman Rockwell," anthologized in *Piety and Politics*, Richard John Neuhaus and Michael Cromartie, eds. (1987), pp. 111-123 and 327-353 respectively.

19. The title of David O. Beale's book is indicative, though the Bob Jones University professor's dates need correction: *In Pursuit of Purity: American Fundamentalism Since* 1850, 1986.

20. Mark G. Toulouse, "J. Frank Norris" in Charles H. Lippy, ed., *Twentieth Century Shapers of American Popular Religion* (New York: Greenwood Press, 1989), p. 311.

21. C. Gwin Morris, "J. Frank Norris and the Baptist General Convention of Texas," *Texas Baptist History*, 1981, pp. 1-34.

22. Baker, A *Baptist Source Book*, p. 196.

23. Toulouse, "J. Frank Norris," p. 315.

24. Ibid, p. 316.

25. SBC TODAY, July 1990, p. 16.

26. See *The Southern Baptist Advocate*, January 1989, p. 3.

27. James C. Hefley, *The Conservative Resurgence in the Southern Baptist Convention* (Hannibal, Missouri: Hannibal Books, 1991), p. 32.

28. *Religious Herald*, September 18, 1980, p. 8.

29. Presnall Wood in *Baptist Standard*, June 20, 1979, p. 6.

30. James C. Hefley, *The Truth in Crisis: The Controversy in the Southern Baptist Convention* (Hannibal, Missouri: Hannibal Books, 1986), p. 65.

31. Robert Tenery, "Remember the Little Red Hen," *Southern Baptist Advocate*, January 1989, p. 3.

32. 1986 SBC *Annual*, p. 37.

33. For more on this section, see SBC TODAY, July 1985, pp. 1, 2.

34. Subsequent to the Dallas Convention, Stanley's ruling and the election of the committee's slate were appealed to the SBC Executive Committee in a series of "bizarre" findings. An expensive lawsuit followed, which did not succeed in overturning the Convention's actions, after the court ruled it did not have jurisdiction in the disagreement.

35. For more on the Elliott controversy, see Walter B. Shurden, *Not a Silent People*, 1972, pp. 103-119. For more on the inerrancy issue, see McBeth,

Baptist Heritage, pp. 680-685.

36. McBeth, Fundamentalism in the SBC in Recent Years," citing Malcolm B. Knight, *Word and Way*, December 20, 1962, p. 5.

37. *The Broadman Bible Commentary*, Vol. 1, 1969, p. 198.

38. To many Southern Baptists, this was like the second book-banning in a decade. Their frustration was intensified by the contrast with some events a year or two earlier. In 1969, Broadman Press published W. A. Criswell's *Why I Preach That the Bible Is Literally True*. Criswell, patriarch of the fundamentalist-tending Southern Baptists, was SBC president in 1969. Broadman Press asked him to write the book and suggested the title. (See W. A. Criswell, *Look Up Brother!*, 1970, p. 68.) The massive promotion given Criswell's 1969 book conveyed the idea that it expressed the official position of the Sunday School Board. One advertisement for the book on the cover of a quarterly for adult Sunday School teachers carried the words, "A book *every* teacher should read." (*Religious Herald*, June 5, 1969, p. 10.)

39. *The Broadman Bible Commentary*, Vol. 1, Revised (Nashville: Broadman Press, 1973).

40. Walter B. Shurden, "The Inerrancy Debate," *Baptist History and Heritage*, April 1981, p. 14.

41. A related piece of dubious history regarding the "Down Grade controversy" among British Baptists is authoritatively rebuffed by Oxford University historian Barrie R. White in his "Open Letter to W. A. Criswell,"

SBC Today, November 1988, p. 16.

42. In a September 3, 1985 letter to David Simpson, then editor of the *Indiana Baptist*, Paul Pressler provides 48 pages of quotations from various authors and speakers. In these pages, Pressler cites *The Battle for the Bible* once as his source. He also includes a half dozen other items that appeared in Lindsell's two books. For a story about seven authors whom Paige Patterson attacked, using some of the same excerpts as are in Lindsell's books, see "Not Guilty: Accused 'Liberals' Deny Charges; Reject Accuser as Authority," *Alabama Baptist*, May 29, 1980, pp. 8-9.

43. McBeth, "Fundamentalism in the SBC in Recent Years," p. 96.

44. The information in this and the next two paragraphs comes from Rob James' telephone interview with James L. Sullivan, former president of the Sunday School Board, January 1, 1989. Sullivan did not name M. O. Owens in the interview, but he acknowledged he had made Owens' identity unmistakable. Quotations in these paragraphs are from *Sojourners*, July 1988, pp. 17-18, which Sullivan confirmed as accurate. Sullivan first presented the material in a May 1986 address to Sunday School Board employees that was published, in part, in *Facts and Trends*.

45. Robinson B. James, ed., *The Unfettered Word: Southern Baptists Confront the Authority-Inerrancy Question* (Waco: Word Books, 1987). This book was republished by Smyth & Helwys Publishing, Inc. with the title, *The Unfettered Word: Confronting the Author-*

ity-Inerrancy Question, in 1994.

46. James pulls the threads of the conference together to show this in *The Unfettered Word*, chapter 12, making use of a key news conference. See the massive *Proceedings of the Conference on Biblical Inerrancy* 1987 (Nashville: Broadman Press, 1987). The papers represented at least three "sides" to the issue, but there is no reference to the most revealing session of all, the news conference with three of the visiting inerrantist experts.

47. For an examination of the historic Baptist position, see W. R. Estep, "Biblical Authority in Baptist Confessions of Faith, 1610-1963," in *The Unfettered Word*, pp. 155-176.

48. Notable resources are Rush Bush and Tom Nettles, *Baptists and the Bible*, 1980 and James Draper, *Authority*, 1984. For a critique of these resources, see *The Unfettered Word*, pp. 91-94, 107-109, 126-127.

49. Around 1890, the youthful Robertson held a Princeton inerrancy position, but moved away from it soon after assuming his New Testament chair in 1895. See Edgar McKnight in *The Unfettered Word*, pp. 99-102.

50. See Edgar V. McKnight, "A. T. Robertson: The Evangelical Middle Is Biblical 'High Ground,'" pp. 90-103; Russell H. Dilday, Jr., "E. Y. Mullins: The Bible's Authority Is a Living, Transforming Reality," pp. 104-124; and Stewart A. Newman, "W. T. Conner: Reason and Freedom, Not Inerrancy," pp. 125-135 in *The Unfettered Word*.

51. Rob James, "Militant Inerrancy Violates Authority Principle of Faith and Message Statement," SBC *Today*, February 1986, p. 8.

52. James Leo Garrett, Jr., "Biblical Authority according to Baptist Confessions of Faith," *Review and Expositor*, Winter 1979, p. 47. Bracketed words added.

53. McBeth, *Baptist Heritage*, p. 685.

54. Fisher Humphreys, "Biblical Inerrancy: A Guide for the Perplexed," quoting L. Russ Bush and Tom J. Nettles, *Baptists and the Bible* (Chicago: Moody Press, 1980), p. 414 in *The Unfettered Word*, p. 51.

55. Kenneth S. Kantzer, "Problems Inerrancy Doesn't Solve," *Christianity Today*, February 20, 1987, p. 15.

56. "Exposition" in *The Chicago Statement of Biblical Inerrancy*, pp. 33-34. See also "Articles of Affirmation and Denial" in the document.

57. *The Chicago Statement on Biblical Inerrancy*, p. 34.

58. For example, Adrian Rogers agreed with Kenneth Kantzer, and H. Edwin Young agreed with J. I. Packer at the 1987 Conference on Biblical Inerrancy at Ridgecrest, *Proceedings of the Conference on Biblical Inerrancy* 1987. pp. 125, 168.

59. "Neo-Orthodoxy Is Problem, No Liberalism, Says Vines," *Baptist Standard*, June 22, 1988, p. 8.

60. Rob James, SBC TODAY, June 1988, p. 4.

61. David S. Dockery, *The Doctrine of the Bible* (Nashville: Convention Press, 1991), pp. 86-88.

62. Clark H. Pinnock, *the Scriptural Principle*, 1984, p. 58.

63. *Proceedings*, p. 75, emphasis added.

64. See Leonard I. Sweet, "Wise as Ser-

pents, Innocent as Doves: The New Evangelical Historiography," *Journal of the American Academy of Religion*, Fall 1988, pp. 397-416.

65. *The Unfettered Word.* pp. 20, 106-107.

66. Russell Dilday, Jr., *The Doctrine of Biblical Authority*, 1982, p. 99.

67. *The Unfettered Word*, p. 124.

68. "Fundamentalism in the SBC in Recent Years," p. 98.

69. "Opening Doors: A brief history of women in ministry in Southern Baptist life, 1868-1993," Louisville: Southern Baptist Women in Ministry, n.d.

70. Ibid.

71. Sarah Frances Anders, "Ordained Women on Rise," BAPTISTS TODAY, March 19, 1998, P. 18.

72. 1994 *Proceedings of the Southern Baptist Convention* (Nashville: Executive Committee, SBC, 1994), p. 65.

73. For another interpretation of 1 Timothy 2:11-15, see Richard and Catherine Clark Kroeger, I *Suffer Not a Woman: Rethinking 1 Timothy 2:11-15 in Light of Ancient Evidence*. Grand Rapids: Baker Book House, 1992. Catherine is founder and president of Christians for Biblical Equality and an adjunct professor at Gordon-Conwell Theological Seminary.

74. SBC TODAY, July 1984, p. 1.

75. July 1994 letter from Southern Baptist Women in Ministry president, Mary B. Zimmer and 1994 "Resolution on Ordination and the Role of Women."

76. SBC TODAY, March-April 1984, p.1.

77. Ibid, December 1983, p. 3.

78. Ibid, June 1984, p. 2.

79. Ibid, March 1985, p. 1.

80. Compiled by Sarah Zimmerman,

BAPTISTS TODAY, September 24, 1998.

81. James W. Watkins, "Stop the Takeover: The Sequel," privately printed pamphlet, 1987.

82. SBC TODAY, November 1986, p. 7.

83. Ibid, November 1986, p. 10.

84. Gustav Niebuhr, "Southern Baptist board defeats effort to aid women pastors," *The Atlanta Journal*, March 12, 1987, p. A31.

85. SBC TODAY, September 1990, p.12.

86. *Southern Baptist Convention Annual, 1988, The Southern Baptist Conventinon*, 1988, p. 156.

87. SBC Convention Bulletin, First Day, Part II, 1987, p. 20.

88. SBC TODAY, July 1987, pp. 1-3. Moderate Cecil E. Sherman had resigned from the committee in October 1986.

89. SBC Convention Bulletin, First Day, Part II, 1987, p. 14.

90. Ibid, p. 12.

91. SBC TODAY, August-September 1987, p. 1.

92. Inter-Office Correspondence, June 24, 1988 and October 30, 1990, on file.

93. SBC TODAY, January 1989, p. 6.

94. Quoted by Doyle Purify, "Texas Minister Cautions Against `Certain Kinds of Fundamentalists,' " BAPTISTS TODAY, May 8, 1997, p. 14.

95. Ibid, quoted from *Baptist Standard*, January 12, 1994.

96. *Baptist Faith and Message*, Section VI, "The Church" (Nashville: Baptist Sunday School Board, 1963), p. 13.

97. *Religious Herald*, January 13, 1994, p. 16.

98. SBC TODAY, July 1988, pp. 1, 3; *Religious Herald*, July 28, 1994, p. 5.

99. Findley Edge, *The Doctrine of the Laity*, 1985; Walter Shurden, *The Doctrine of the Priesthood of Believers*, 1987; Herschel Hobbs, *The Baptist Faith and Message*, 1971. pp. 8-12.

100. E. Y. Mullins, *The Axioms of Religion*, 1908, pp. 72-74, 94, 95, 106, 107.

101. W. T. Conner, *Christian Doctrine* (Nashville: Broadman Press, 1937), p. 268.

102. *Baptist Ideals* (Nashville: Sunday School Board, n.d.), p. 6.

103. William C. Boone, *What We Believe* (Nashville: Convention Press, 1936), p. 71.

104. The Fellowship Covenant: Second Baptist Church, Hot Springs Arkansas, p. 2.

105. SBC TODAY, July 1984, p. 3.

106. *Sojourners*, July 1988, p. 21.

107. SBC TODAY, March 1985, p. 1.

108. *Sojourners*, July 1988, p. 21.

109. SBC TODAY, December 1987, p. 8.

110. *Sojourners*, July 1988, p. 21.

111. SBC TODAY, February 1989, P. 3.

112. Ibid, April 1989, p. 7.

113. "Agency defers accreditation act on SEBTS," SBC TODAY, April 1990, p. 23.

114. SBC TODAY, August 1990, p. 7.

115. "Association gives 'Warning' to Southeastern Seminary," SBC TODAY, February 1990, p. 11.

116. SBC TODAY, August 9, 1991, p. 3.

117. "Southeastern trustees set inerrancy in documents," BAPTISTS TODAY, October 31, 1991, p. 4.

118. Lisa Bellany, "Southeastern denies Drummond chancellorship, sabbatical," BAPTISTS TODAY, April 2, 1992, p. 13.

119. BAPTISTS TODAY, May 28, 1992, p. 11.

120. Ibid, July 16, 1992, p. 2.

121. "ATS Notifies Southeastern Accreditation Is Reaffirmed," *The Christian Index*, July 7, 1994, p. 3.

122. BAPTISTS TODAY, August 20, 1992, p. 3.

123. "SEBTS celebrates endowment; trustees OK curriculum changes," *Baptists Today*, April 14, 1994, p. 13.

124. "Fundamentalists take control of trustees at Southern Baptist Theological Seminary," SBC TODAY, June 1990, p. 3.

125. "Seminary president Honeycutt responds to charges of trustees," SBC TODAY, June 1990, p. 3.

126. Greg Warner, "Al Mohler is nominee for Southern presidency," *Baptists Today*, March 4, 1993, p. 5.

127. "Southern trustees refuse endowed chairs to professors," *Baptists Today*, May 13, 1993, p. 1.

128. Marv Knox, "Southern discontinues exhibits, alumni meetings at Fellowship," BAPTISTS TODAY, February 17, 1994, p. 1.

129. *Religious Herald*, September 1, 1994, p. 12.

130. "Trustees affirm Mohler, grant more authority over faculty," BAPTISTS TODAY, May 4, 1995, p. 1.

131. *Religious Herald*, April 25, 1996, p. 9.

132. Mark Wingfield, "Longtime Southern Seminary Librarian Fired After Challenging SBC Leader," BAPTISTS TODAY, October 16, 1997, p. 25.

133. "Gains by conservatives far exceed call for `balance' struck in 1991," Associated Baptist Press, April 23, 1998.

134. Ibid, June 6, 1996, p.5.

135. "Dilday, trustees reach compromise," SBC TODAY, November 1989, p.1.

136. "Southwestern seminary rated tops in USA," SBC TODAY, April 1990, p. 23.

137. "Dilday clarifies statement," SBC TODAY, August 1990, p. 9.

138. "Southwestern seminary trustees adopt budget, evaluate Dilday," BAPTISTS TODAY, April 1, 1993, p. 5.

139. Jack U. Harwell, "A tragic event in theological history," BAPTISTS TODAY, March 24, 1994, p. 6.

140. "Fallout growing from Dilday firing," BAPTISTS TODAY, April 28, 1994, p. 6.

141. Toby Druin and Greg Warner, "Students left to wonder, 'Why? Why?'" BAPTISTS TODAY, March 24, 1994, p. 10.

142. "Trustees rush to justify Dilday firing as outraged Baptists withhold money," BAPTISTS TODAY, April 14, 1994, pp. 1, 3, 5.

143. Letter on file.

144. "Dilday 'appalled' by letters' 'inaccuracies, distortions'," The Baptist Standard, April 6, 1994, p. 4.

145. "An Open Letter to Southern Baptists," The Baptist Standard, April 20, 1994, p. 21.

146. "Southwestern warned to act to avert probation," Religious Herald, August 4, 1994, p. 8.

147. Religious Herald, July 21, 1994, p. 7.

148. "Southwestern Gets Probation from ATS Accrediting Agency," Christian Index, February 9, 1995, pp. 2, 3.

149. "Southwestern trustees elect Hemphill to succeed Dilday," Florida Baptist Witness, August 4, 1994, p. 4; "Hemphill addresses constituencies; concerns at Southwestern Seminary," Ibid, p. 5.

150. "Dilday accepts job with Truett Seminary," Florida Baptist Witness, August 4, 1994, p. 6.

151. Bob Allen, "Mark Coppenger Calls Women Preachers 'Affront to Home and Family'," BAPTISTS TODAY, May 23, 1996, p. 8.

152. "Midwestern trustees block faculty recommendations," BAPTISTS TODAY, May 13, 1993, p. 1.

153. Bob Terry, "Stancil denied tenure over inerrancy issue," BAPTISTS TODAY, November 11, 1993, p. 3.

154. "Mark Coppenger Elected President of Midwestern," Christian Index, June 15, 1995, p. 28.

155. "Virginia Midwestern Alumni Chapter Questions Mark Coppenger Statements," BAPTISTS TODAY, February 8, 1996, p. 19.

156. New England Baptist, July 1998, p. 2.

157. "Landrum Leavell stuns seminary with end-of-year retirement," BAPTISTS TODAY, January 5, 1995, p.3.

158. "Kelley elected at New Orleans," Baptist Standard, February 28, 1996, p. 4.

159. Lacy Thompson, "Pastors Denied Teaching Posts Over Their Ties to Fellowship," BAPTISTS TODAY, August 21, 1997, p. 3.

160. Wayne Nicholson, Columbus, Oh., in a guest editorial in BAPTISTS TODAY, March 19, 1998, P. 7.

161. Alister E. McGrath, Christian Theology: An Introduction (Cambridge, Mass.: Basil Blackwell Inc., 1994), p. 398.

162. "'Founders' group works to pre-

serve Calvinism in Southern Baptist Life," BAPTISTS TODAY, February 16, 1995, pp. 4-5.

163. "History Professor Disputes Calvinism of Early Baptists," *Christian Index*, May 1, 1997, pp. 10-11.

164. For more on the difference between a Calvinist and a faithful and free Baptist, read Bill Bruster's "Is Your Church Free or Reformed? This pamphlet is available from the Cooperative Baptist Fellowship.

165. *Associated Baptist Press*, June 29, 1998.

166. Promotional material, "Wake Forest University Divinity School, n.d.

167. "Wake Forest gets grants to shape divinity school," *Florida Baptist Witness*, May 26, 1994, p. 10.

168. "Baylor creates separate system for governance," SBC TODAY, November 2, 1990, p. 2.

169. *The Baptist Standard*, April 20, 1994, p. 22; Toby Druin, "If demand is there, Baylor to expand Truett." *The Baptist Standard*, May 25, 1994, p.4.

170. "Furman trustees change charter, anger Baptists," SBC TODAY, November 2, 1990, p. 17.

171. "Samford gets $38.8 million gift," SBC TODAY, December 15, 1990, p. 2.

172. "Mississippi College trustees back off secession vote," BAPTISTS TODAY, November 10, 1994, p. 2.

173. "Carson-Newman trustees vote to elect successors," *Baptist & Reflector*, April 22, 1998, p. 1.

174. "Gardner-Webb plans school of divinity," BAPTISTS TODAY, September 24, 1992, p. 17.

175. "HSU to offer M. Div. degree," *The*

Baptist Standard, May 25, 1994, p. 4.

176. William Neal, "Mercer Trustees Approve School of Theology," *The Christian Index*, July 7, 1994, pp. 1-2.

177. *Christian Index*, May 1, 1997, p. 1.

178. "New Virginia School," *Religious Herald*, February 5, 1998, p. 4.

179. "Campbellsville offers new master's degree," *Western Recorder*, March 10, 1998, p. 3.

180. Mark Wingfield, "New Kentucky seminary envisioned in Georgetown," *Western Recorder*, August 11, 1998, p. 3.

181. Don McGregor, "New Commission Unreasonable," SBC TODAY, March 1989, p. 8.

182. *The Baptist Standard*, September 16, 1987, p. 2.

183. Jack U. Harwell, "Liberty commission dead; CLC given church-state lead," SBC TODAY, October 1989, p. 2.

184. Michael Smith, "BJC Freedom Fighters Thrive Despite Assaults," BAPTISTS TODAY, August 20, 1998, p. 4, quoting *The New York Times*, March 23, 1998.

185. "Baker Replaces Valentine at CLC," SBC TODAY, February 1987, p. 3.

186. "Baker Holds on to CLC Post in 15-15 Vote of Confidence," SBC TODAY, October 1987, p. 7.

187. "Texas CLC Rejects Views," *Baptist Standard*, September 28, 1988, p.4.

188. *Religious Herald*, December 1, 1988, p. 10.

189. "CLC Commissioners Issue Statement on Race," *Religious Herald*, February 9, 1989, p. 10; "CLC and

Land emphasize race relations," SBC TODAY, March 1989, p. 1.

190. Greg Warner, "Moderate Baptists form ethics agency with 'different focus' from SBC CLC," BAPTISTS TODAY, August 9, 1991, p. 4.

191. Mark Wingfield, "Presidential Hopefuls Seek Blessing from Religious Right at Memphis Rally," BAPTISTS TODAY, February 8, 1996, p. 3.

192. Guy Gugliotta, "GOP Moves to Bolster Ties to Evangelicals," *The Washington Post*, May 9, 1998.

193. "BSSB trustees turn aside attempt to fire Elder," SBC TODAY, September 1989, p. 1.

194. "Sunday School Board trustees refuse to print their history," SBC TODAY, September 1990, p. 4.

195. "Faculty affirms McBeth and book killed by BSSB," SBC TODAY, October 1990, p. 2.

196. Darrell Turner, "Lloyd Elder to retire at Baptist Sunday School Board," SBC TODAY, February 8, 1991, pp. 1-2.

197. "Baptist Board president agrees to teach at Belmont," *Nashville Banner*, June 12, 1991, p. B-2.

198. "Draper wins easy election to Sunday School Board," BAPTISTS TODAY, August 9, 1991, p. 14.

199. Ray Waddle, "Advanced retirement for 150 Sunday School Board employees," BAPTISTS TODAY, November 26, 1992, p. 4.

200. W. G. Stracener, "Every Baptist has right, responsibility to know," Reprinted in *Florida Baptist Witness*, August 13, 1998, p. 3.

201. SBC *Annual*, 1987, p. 230.

202. RNA *Newsletter*, September/October 1988.

203. "Leaders of Baptist Press terminated; editors start new press association," SBC TODAY, August 1990, p. 1.

204. Ibid.

205. Ibid, p. 31.

206. "McGregor is executive director of Associated Baptist Press," SBC TODAY, March 8, 1991, p. 1.

207. "Warner is full-time editor Associated Baptist Press," SBC TODAY, May 3, 1991, p. 1.

208. "Texas anti-gambling group named Dan Martin director," BAPTISTS TODAY, January 9, 1993, p. 5.

209. Jack E. Brymer, Sr., "Baptist journalism needs more, not less investigative reporting," *Florida Baptist Witness*, March 3, 1994, p. 7.

210. "CLC criticizes North Carolina editor," *Florida Baptist Witness*, April 14, 1994, p. 15.

211. Jack E. Brymer, Sr., "The good news is not so good," *Florida Baptist Witness*, June 16, 1994, p. 7; "SBC official blast Baptist media for coverage of Dilday firing," *Florida Baptist Witness*, June 16, 1994, pp. 6-7; Art Toalston, "Coppenger targets Baptist media as biased," *Religious Herald*, June 9, 1994, pp. 10-11; "Press association president responds to Coppenger article," *Religious Herald*, June 9, 1994, p. 11.

212. *Religious Herald*, September 1, 1994, p. 11.

213. "Tenery resigns North Carolina pastorate," SBC TODAY, November 16, 1990, p. 2.

214. "Fundamentalist magazine dropped by Jerry Falwell," SBC TODAY, January 1990, p. 22.

215. "New fundamentalist newspaper," BAPTISTS TODAY, December 19, 1991, p. 7.

216. Steve Fox, "Samford University survives a close call," BAPTISTS TODAY, January 9, 1993, p. 10.

217. "Baptist Banner trustees elect associate editor," Religious Herald, May 12, 1994, p. 11.

218. "Parks retirement as FMB president ends era of global mission advance," BAPTISTS TODAY, November 12, 1992, p. 6.

219. "Missionary Asked to Resign," SBC TODAY, August 1988, pp. 1, 2, 17.

220. "Willett Terminated by FMB," SBC TODAY, September 1988, pp. 1, 2.

221. "FMB chair affirms Parks, reveals Lottie Moon plan," SBC TODAY, September 1990, p. 11.

222. Robert Dilday, "FMB drops funding for Swiss seminary; European Baptist leaders react angrily," BAPTISTS TODAY, October 31, 1991, pp. 1, 3.

223. "N.C. Baptist Men to coordinate seminary relocation," Religious Herald, June 9, 1994, p. 12.

224. Robert Dilday, "Parks, FMB trustees avoid conflict over his tenure," BAPTISTS TODAY, October 31, 1991, pp. 1, 4, 7.

225. Greg Warner, "FMB's Keith Parks to retire citing leadership concerns," BAPTISTS TODAY, April 2, 1992, p. 1.

226. "Parks faces FMB trustees over decisions," BAPTISTS TODAY, February 6, 1992, p. 1.

227. "Parks retirement as FMB president ends era of global mission advance," BAPTISTS TODAY, November 12, 1992, p. 6.

228. Greg Warner, "Elliff turns down offer to become FMB president," BAPTISTS TODAY, February 18, 1993, p. 2.

229. Greg Warner, "'Dark Horse' Jerry Rankin chosen as FMB nominee," Baptists Today, June 29, 1993, p. 2.

230. Walter Shurden, Not a Silent People: Controversies that Have Shaped Southern Baptists, Smyth & Helwys, 1995, p. 91.

231. James H. Slatton, "The History of the Moderate Political Network," in The Struggle for the Soul of the SBC:Moderate Responses to the Fundamentalist Movement, edited by Walter Shurden, Smyth & Helwys, 1993, p. 50.

232. Grady C. Cothen, What Happened to the Southern Baptist Convention: A Memoir of the Controversy, Smyth & Helwys, 1993, pp. 255-256.

233. Slatton, The Struggle for the Soul of the SBC, edited by Walter Shurden, p. 50.

234. Cecil Sherman, "An Overview of the Moderate Movement," in The Struggle for the Soul of the SBC, edited by Walter Shurden, Smyth & Helwys, 1993, pp. 23, 40 and 42.

235. Southern Baptist Alliance Constitution and By-Laws, Article 2.

236. Amy Greene, "SBA looks to future, drops 'Southern' name," BAPTISTS TODAY, March 19, 1992, p. 1. Persons may write to the Alliance of Baptists at 1328 16th Street, N.W., Washington, D.C. 20036.

237. "Alliance Formed to Preserve SBC Threatened Heritage," SBC news release of February 11, 1987, with attachments.

238. "Minutes of the Board of Directors

Meeting, SBA, November 28-29, 1988," plus notes of Rob James from that meeting and the meeting of the same board on March 1, 1989, in Greenville, South Carolina. See also "Alliance Takes Great Strides," SBC TODAY, January 1989, p. 1.

239. "Richmond Baptist seminary sets covenant, moves office," BAPTISTS TODAY, August 23, 1991, P. 3.

240. Alan Neely, A New Call to Mission: Help for Perplexed Churches, Published by the Alliance of Baptists, Washington, D.C., 1999, pp. 48-49.

241. Pam Parry, "Alliance evaluates future, plans study of sexuality," BAPTISTS TODAY, October 14, 1993, p. 1.

242. Gary Parker, "Being Baptist in 21st Century Means Standing for Principles," BAPTISTS TODAY, September 18, 1997, p. 19.

243. Jack U. Harwell, "Fundamentalist steamroller flattens SBC in New Orleans; moderates ponder options," SBC TODAY, July 1990, p. 1.

244. Jack U. Harwell, " Moderates create new funding mechanism for SBC fellowship; set spring convocation," SBC TODAY, September 1990, p. 1.

245. Amy Greene, "Cooperative Fellowship formed in Atlanta," SBC TODAY, May 31, 1991, p. 1.

246. Jack U. Harwell, "CBF calls Sherman; will fund Europeans," BAPTISTS TODAY, January 23, 1992, p. 1; "Sherman accepts CBF post as coordinator," BAPTISTS TODAY, February 6, 1992, p. 1.

247. "SBC leaders convince agencies to cancel Fellowship exhibits," BAPTISTS TODAY, April 23, 1992, p. 15.

248. Steve Wright, "The battle of wills: WMU 1, fundamentalists 0," BAPTISTS TODAY, April 14, 1994, p. 8.

249. Jack Harwell, "President Carter and others laud election of Keith Parks," BAPTISTS TODAY, January 9, 1993, p. 1.

250. Jack Harwell, "CBF sets new mission strategy; elects Law," BAPTISTS TODAY, March 4, 1993, p. 1.

251. Greg Warner, "CBF support strong in traditional SBC states," BAPTISTS TODAY, March 10, 1994, p. 6.

252. Cecil Sherman, "About homosexuality," BAPTISTS TODAY, April 1, 1994, p. 23.

253. Greg Warner, "Fellowship names 10 missionaries," Religious Herald, May 12, 1994, p. 3.

254. "Vestal sounds theme of freedom after election as CBF executive," Religious Herald, October 3, 1996, p. 10.

255. BAPTISTS TODAY, May 21, 1998, pp. 10-11.

256. "Cecil P. Staton, Jr., "Publisher explains linkage of Smyth & Helwys, Mercer," BAPTISTS TODAY, October 31, 1991, p. 2.

257. "Smyth & Helwys materials lauded," BAPTISTS TODAY, February 18, 1993, p. 13.

258. Mark Kelly, "SBC now 'on trial,' Clinton's pastor says," Baptists Today, July 29, 1993, p. 10.

259. Offset on file.

260. "Controversial paper's distribution was unauthorized, Patterson says," Baptists Today, June 29, 1993, p. 5.

261. Letter on file.

262. Melvin Cammack, *John Wyclif and the English Bible* (New York: American Tract Society, 1938), p. 75.

263. BAPTISTS TODAY, May 12, 1994, pp. 1, 5.

264. *Baptist Standard*, June 22, 1994, p.5.

265. *Religious Herald*, June 23, 1994, p. 7; *The Baptist Standard*, June 29, 1994, p. 3.

266. "CBF officers curtail two giving plans," BAPTISTS TODAY, August 18, 1994, p. 1.

267. BAPTISTS TODAY, July 14, 1994, p. 8.

268. *Baptist Standard*, June 22, 1994, p.6.

269. *Baptist Standard*, August 17, 1994, p. 13.

270. "Tarheel leader predicts response if funds cut, Reminds HMB partnership is for cooperation, not control," *The Baptist Standard*, July 20, 1994, p. 12.

271. Robert Dilday, "Virginia's budget options cloud ties of local churches to national SBC," BAPTISTS TODAY, January 9, 1993, p. 3.

272. *Religious Herald*, November 3, 1994, p. 5.

273. Ibid, July 21, 1994, p.8.

274. "Conservative group votes Virginia split," *Baptist Standard*, September 25, 1996, pp. 1, 3.

275. "Fundamental-conservative leaders meet with Fred Wolfe," *Word & Way*, March 4, 1994, p. 6.

276. "Convention chartered in Texas," BAPTISTS TODAY, November 10, 1994, p. 7.

277. "Texas fundamentalists vow to organize opposition," BAPTISTS TODAY, November 30, 1994, p. 4.

278. Toby Druin, "Southern Baptists of Texas look to November," *Baptist Standard*, May 6, 1998, p. 3.

279. "Alabama conservatives meet, elect steering committee," *The Alabama Baptist*, April 30, 1998, p. 16.

280. "'Mainstream Missouri Baptists' opposes Project 1000," *Word & Way*, August 13, 1998, p. 3.

281. "CBF ties lead to removal," *Baptist Standard*, January 5, 1994, p. 4.

282. William Neal, "Historical Plan Restructures SBC, *Christian Index*, March 2, 1995, pp. 1-3.

283. *Christian Index*, May 4, 1995, p. 5.

284. "Brotherhood Trustees Decline to 'Embrace' Restructuring," *Christian Index*, May 4, 1995, p.5.

285. Harold Shirley, "South Carolina Minister Says Slandering of Woman's Missionary Union Symptomatic," BAPTISTS TODAY, April 17, 1997, p. 11.

286. John F.Baugh, *The Battle for Baptist Integrity*, Battle for Baptist Integrity inc., 1997, p. 111.

287. Bob Allen, "Rankin Decries WMU Move to Publish Materials for CBF," *Christian Index*, September 7, 1995, p. 8.

288. *Christian Index*, March 9, 1995, p. 3.

289. James C. Hefley, *Issues & Effects: The Controversy Between "Conservatives" & "Moderates" in the Southern Baptist Convention* (Hannibal, Mo.: Hannibal Books, 1998), p.11.

290. "Return to power," *Religious Herald*, June 6, 1996, p. 4. Although Henry was not the hand picked candidate of the Takeover faction, when James Hefley needed the name of a pastor of a fundamentalist church which strongly supported the Cooperative Program, he chose

Henry, not any of the hardline fundamentalist pastors. With their independent, non-cooperative mindset, they have not traditionally been strong supporters of the Cooperative Program.

291. Greg Warner, "SBC leaders draw tighter circle," *Baptist Standard*, June 5, 1996, p. 3.

292. "The SBC responds," *Religious Herald*, June 20, 1996, p. 2.

293. "The SBC responds," *Religious Herald*, June 20, 1996, p. 1.

294. 'An insult to Jewish people,' *Religious Herald*, July 18, 1996, p. 4.

295. Pat Anderson, "Pat Anderson Questions Southern Baptist Resolution Suggesting Boycott of Disney Corporation Products," BAPTISTS TODAY, July 24, 1997, p. 12.

296. Willian Neal, "Disney Boycott Overshadows Convention," *Christian Index*, June 26, 1997, p. 4.

297. *The Christian Index*, June 25, 1998, p. 1.

298. *The Charlotte Observer*, June 6, 1998, p. 1G.

299. Quoted by Marse Grant in "The Saga of Jerry Falwell: Did He Join the Southern Baptist Convention?" BAPTIST TODAY, January 9, 1997, p. 15.

300. Ibid.

301. *Word & Way*, June 18, 1998, p. 16.

302. *Western Recorder*, June 16, 1998, p.6.

303. *Word & Way*, April 2, 1998, p. 16.

304. "Jerry Falwell to appear at SBC gathering," *Biblical Recorder*, March 14, 1998, p. 2.

305. Toby A. Druin, "Hopefuls may have to yield to Falwell," *Baptist Standard*, July 15, 1998, p. 4.

306. "Falwell Joins Southern Baptist Convention," *The Sword of the Lord*, August 7, 1998, pp. 1, 4, 6.

307. *Word & Way*, June 18, 1998, p. 3.

308. *Western Recorder*, June 16, 1998, p. 5.

309. Michael Chute, "Baptist Faith and Message Study Authorized" in *The Florida Baptist Witness*, June 24, 1999, p. 1.

310. *Baptist New Mexican*, June 20, 1998, p. 8.

311. *Western Recorder*, June 16, 1998, p. 10; *Religious Herald*, June 18, 1998, p. 8.

312. Toby A. Druin, "Hopefuls may have to yield to Falwell," *Baptist Standard*, July 15, 1998, p. 4.

313. "Inerrancy affirmation only first step in SBC reformation, pastor declares," Baptist Press, March 16, 1998.

314. "Biblical preaching is expository, Calvinists contend," *Western Recorder*, August 11, 1998, p. 2.

315. *Religious Herald*, March 9, 1989, pp. 5, 9.

316. Dan Martin, "Texas Baptists Committed explores servant leadership," *Baptist Standard*, June 15, 1994, p. 8.

Index of Names

About the Authors

Robison James, Ph.D.

Robison James is a graduate of Southern Baptist Theological Seminary (BD), with a Ph.D degree from Duke University. Before going to University of Richmond, he was pastor of churches in Alabama, Kentucky and Virginia. Dr. James was a member of the Virginia General Assembly from 1976-1983. He is also editor and main author of *The Unfettered Word: Southern Baptists Confront the Authority - Inerrancy Question* (Word Books, 1987).

Gary Leazer, Ph.D.

Gary Leazer is a graduate of Mississippi College (BA) and Southwestern Baptist Theological Seminasry (MDiv and PhD) Degrees. He has done additional graduate study at North Texas State University and the University of Iowa. In 1979 – the same year the SBC controversy "officially" started in Houston – Dr. Leazer became assistant director of the Interfaith Witness Department of the SBC Home Mission Board. He became director of the department in 1987.

In 1992-93, he conducted the controversial SBC investigation of Freemasonry and, in 1993, was dismissed by the board after he spoke to a Masonic group to explain the meaning of the 1993 SBC action on the fraternity.

In 1994, Dr. Leazer started the Center for Interfaith Studies, Inc., in Stone Mountain, GA. He continues to lead conferences and produces a quarterly newsletter on interfaith subjects. In 1998, he served as interim associate editor of BAPTISTS TODAY.

James G. Shoopman, Ph.D.

Dr. Jim Shoopman serves as the Pastor of Indigo Lakes Baptist Church in Daytona Beach, Florida. He has served on the Representative Assembly of the Cooperative Baptist Fellowship of Florida, and still serves on the Education Ministry Group for that body. He was born in 1954, raised in rural southern Arkansas and in Clearwater, Florida. Dr. Shoopman earned a Bachelors Degree in English from Stetson University in 1977, and then graduated from New Orleans Baptist Theological Seminary with a major in Biblical studies in 1983. Following service on the staff of the Baptist Association of Greater New Orleans for three years, he earned his Ph.D. in Humanities in 1994, with a concentration in religious studies at Florida State University in Tallahassee, where he focused on the sociology and history of American religion. While in Florida he has served as a Pastor, an Associate Pastor and an Interim Pastor in recent years. He is married to the former Susan Haywood Euson, through whom he enjoys two grown step-daughters and a grandson.